THE SPOONRIVER COOKBOOK

THE SPOONRIVER COOKBOOK

BRENDA LANGTON AND MARGARET STUART

PHOTOGRAPHS BY METTE NIELSEN

University of Minnesota Press   MINNESOTA   MINNEAPOLIS // LONDON

Frontispiece photograph by Travis Anderson

Photographs on pages xii, xiii, 141, and 143 courtesy of Brenda Langton

Photograph on page 161 courtesy of Suzanne Weinstein

Published by the University of Minnesota Press
111 Third Avenue South, Suite 290
Minneapolis, MN 55401-2520
http://www.upress.umn.edu

A Cataloging-in-Publication record is available from the Library of Congress.
ISBN 978-0-8166-7628-6

Printed in China on acid-free paper

The University of Minnesota is an equal-opportunity educator and employer.

19 18 17 16 15 14 13 12   10 9 8 7 6 5 4 3 2 1

CONTENTS

ACKNOWLEDGMENTS

I WOULD LIKE TO ACKNOWLEDGE those who have been inspiration to my work and contributed to the creation of this book.

Thank you to my team of talented cooks, kitchen staff, and front of house staff who are dedicated to bringing beautiful healthy food to our customers day after day. I am extremely grateful for the soul they bring to Spoonriver through their innovation, dedication, and pride in their work and the restaurant.

A very special thanks to Timothy Kane, my husband, business partner, and constant supporter. As partners in life, we've found the right recipe to keep things savory and sweet. Tim keeps all operational ingredients in line, with just the right amount of seasoning. His endless under-the-radar efforts make Spoonriver possible.

To chef Liz Benser, who has been by my side for twenty-five years, creating beautiful seafood and vegetarian specials night after night.

To chef Chris Bundy for his innovative dishes and incredible dedication.

To chef Heather Hartman, the queen of vegetarian specials and Mill City Farmers Market chef.

To chef Nick Schneider, who has blossomed into a wise and wonderful cook and grower of what we eat.

To chef Stephanie Wourms, who makes the most beautiful steak plates with a rainbow of market vegetables and scrumptious sauces.

To our beautiful Zoila Gonzalez, composing our lovely salads, sandwiches, and more with her magic touch.

To all of the farmers, producers, and purveyors who supply me with the freshest produce and highest-quality meats, specialty products, and unique ingredients that make my recipes and menus possible. It has been a great honor to bring the Mill City Farmers Market into our backyard to educate our community about healthy foods and local farmers.

To Peggy Stuart, my dear friend since adolescence, who coauthored *The Cafe Brenda Cookbook* and now our Spoonriver collection.

To Todd Orjala at the University of Minnesota Press, a huge fan who understands who I am and why we cook the way we do. His editorial expertise was invaluable.

To Jane Cutler, who knows me so damn well.

And finally, to our customers, who paid as they could at Commonplace in the early seventies, who streamed in on May Day in 1978 when we first opened the door of Cafe Kardamena, who contributed to our nearly quarter century at Cafe Brenda, and who are now present at our 100-foot-long communal table, Spoonriver. To each of you I say *thank you!* Knowing that the results of our hard work reach and teach so many people is extremely gratifying. When our customers tell me that eating at Cafe Kardamena, Cafe Brenda, or Spoonriver made them "feel good all day" I feel that I have accomplished my life's work.

Brenda Langton
MARCH 2012

INTRODUCTION //

GROWING UP, my favorite meal was boiled dinner. My mother worked, yet all our meals were made from scratch because that was most economical and, frankly, she was of a generation that wouldn't have considered doing it any other way. When I reflect on my childhood love of boiled dinner, I realize that it was what accompanied the ham that appealed to me—the cabbage, potatoes, and onions. I'd already sensed in a meat-and-potatoes world that animal protein didn't have to dominate to satisfy. A shift away from meat as the primary source of protein on the dinner plate is beginning to catch on, and a return to the kitchen, where America has spent on average half an hour per day, is becoming more of a priority, even among working parents. The things we've been putting in our bodies have been making us sick; we can no longer afford to ignore that we are what we eat. There's a sense of urgency in the air, and now is the time to get on board! The whole-foods revolution is finally going mainstream, as evidenced in the proliferation of farmers' markets, community gardens, and more shelf space for organic products.

I joined the revolution, immersing myself in the cooperative food movement at an early age. And I do mean early. I was fifteen years old when I peered through the windows of a restaurant under construction in my St. Paul neighborhood, walked in, and applied for a job. It was there, at Commonplace Cooperative Restaurant, that my education in plant-based proteins like whole grains, nuts, and legumes began and my life was forever changed. I discovered a new direction in eating and food preparation that was really steeped in tradition. It harkened back to prewar times, before the processed foods that promised to simplify life and reduce time in the kitchen robbed our culture of a more wholesome sensibility about nutrition. We had moved away from whole foods, vegetable gardens, canning our own produce, and savoring the warmth of the kitchen. As a nation, we've paid the price in epidemic obesity and chronic illnesses like diabetes, cancer, and heart disease. Good old Commonplace was crazy and energizing. Sure, it had its share of long-haired men in skirts, but there was also foresight and real dedication in the people who worked there, riffing on the cookbooks fast filtering in from the coasts. Most important, Commonplace kick-started me on my life's path. My mother, were she still alive, would be amazed! Her headstrong, little hippie daughter had been onto something from the get-go.

It's been nearly forty years since I joined the counterculture, and my three successful and award-winning restaurants have all taken their cues from those wild days of my

Commonplace Specials

Stir-fried Tofu, Rice, & Vegetables *with Sweet & Sour or Non-Dairy Curry Nut Sauce*	3.00
Egg Foo Yong *with fresh sprouts, tamari, garlic & ginger sauce, and Rice*	2.50
Vegetable Sukiyaki *fresh vegetables in a delicately seasoned sauce over rice*	2.50
Price includes Soup or Salad & Tea	
Mushroom Croquettes & Bread *with Cheddar Cheese Sauce*	3.00
Bean Enchiladas *in a sweet chile sauce & rice*	2.50
Cheese Enchiladas *Refried Beans or Rice*	2.75
Guacamole Sprout Toastadas *Refried Beans & Rice*	2.75

House Dressings: Oil, Vinegar & Herbs   French
Honey-Ginger   Cheese-Garlic   Tahini-Tamari

Brenda at Cafe Kardamena, 1978
Menu from Commonplace Cooperative Restaurant,
St. Paul, 1974

youth. Cafe Kardamena, my first, was both an outgrowth of my early experience and an inspiration that arose from a year of travel in Europe, where the gorgeous markets and restaurants that sourced their foods locally and seasonally were the major attraction for me. Although my then boyfriend, Timothy, who is a painter, dragged me through every museum, church, and monument, I was much more interested in scouring our guidebooks for healthy, wholesome ethnic cooking to eat. I came back ready to elevate what I'd learned at Commonplace with the lessons I'd learned in Europe. Kardamena was no brown rice and veggies joint. What we served in our small St. Paul space was gourmet vegetarian and fresh seafood cuisine. We found that people were clamoring to eat well and healthfully, so much so that we had to look for more square footage

after eight years on Cathedral Hill. An inspiring trip to California that featured meals at the iconic Greens in San Francisco and a visit with Alice Waters and a delicious dinner at Chez Panisse further impelled us to create a more beautiful and visible restaurant that would reach more people. I had always seen Cafe Kardamena as a stepping-stone, and I was pretty fearless in stepping off, happy to be moving along to new adventures.

At the insistence of Timothy, now my husband and business partner, our new restaurant in the warehouse district of downtown Minneapolis took my name. Cafe Brenda

Brenda with her husband, Timothy Kane, and daughter, Celina, outside Cafe Brenda during the closing gala, December 9, 2009.

quickly became a top Twin Cities destination for casual fine dining with an emphasis on gourmet natural foods. We built a beautiful restaurant that had large Palladian windows surrounding the dining room, and it didn't feel anything like the Earth Shoe, hanging-fern restaurants one might expect with this genre of food. The menu always included a vegetarian plate we called *Sozai* or, translated from the Japanese, "today's meal." We offered fresh fish entrées and farm-fresh chicken and continued with our philosophy of promoting the health benefits of plant-based proteins with entrées like Buckwheat Sweet Potato Croquettes that customers went nuts for. I shopped the Minneapolis Farmers Market with my baby daughter, Celina, strapped to me and delivered the freshest ingredients to the Cafe Brenda kitchen, building delicious spe-

cials around the vegetables spilling from my basket. My daughter was virtually raised at Cafe Brenda, so when we decided to move on after twenty-three years, she really mourned. The restaurant had been her home and her family. On closing night, Celina delivered a farewell tribute that brought the house to tears. But we all knew it was time to go, time to realize a new vision in a new setting.

When I came up with the name Spoon-river, everyone I ran it by followed with, Anthology? I had never heard of *Spoon River Anthology*. I liked the name Spoon, but Alain Ducasse had already nabbed that, in Paris.

The bar at Spoonriver

We were going to be located next to the new Guthrie Theater on the Mississippi River, and acknowledging our proximity to the river seemed an obvious choice. I call Spoonriver my little train car because the space is long and narrow, 11 by 100 feet, and because it's located in the historic Mill District, once busy with trains hauling grain from all over the Midwest. Huge windows (just like those we loved at Cafe Brenda) onto the street fill Spoonriver with light. All my restaurants have been so special to me, but this one is the most beautiful. With this new beginning, I was able to expand my repertoire and give our loyal and growing clientele what had in the past ten years become available in an ever-evolving world of natural foods—meat! The Spoonriver menu includes grass-fed beef, naturally raised lamb and pork, and free-range chicken. These are not the products of feedlots and inhumane treatment. We have

wonderful relationships with all of our local farmers. We know where and how the animals that provide our meat were raised.

Spoonriver patrons can buy from some of the very same vendors at the Mill City Market that takes place every Saturday, May through October, right outside the restaurant door. For me, the creation of the market alongside the restaurant is a dream pairing, the epitome of the farm-to-table experience. Our market features local growers and meat and dairy producers offering the highest-quality products—many organic—in a lovely setting. It's inspiring shopping. You see friends; build relationships with vendors; grab a bite to eat at a market stall, food truck, or the restaurant; listen to live music. You fill your bags with beautiful

Dining al fresco at Spoonriver next to the Guthrie Theater

goods and take them home to your kitchen, energized in a way that just doesn't compare with a trip to the grocery store. While it's impossible for most to access a farmers' market year-round, excellent produce and other staples can be found in your community food co-op and in the organic sections of your grocery store. Healthy ingredients for your everyday cooking are now widely available, and while I urge you to support farmers' markets and local producers who employ sustainable farming methods, sometimes we just have to go outside our regions to feed our families.

I always rely on the freshest local and organic produce, dairy, and other ingredients as the foundation for our delicious and healthy seasonal menus during the growing season, and so can you. Cooking appetizing, wholesome food doesn't have to be intimidating or expensive. The recipes included in *The Spoonriver Cookbook* are easy to prepare and include one-pot dishes, simple and tasty vegetable sides, legume recipes, and whole-grain preparations. *The Spoonriver Cookbook* features a broader palate than its predecessor, *The Cafe Brenda Cookbook,* as this new collection follows the expansion of our latest restaurant's offerings. But it also revisits and enhances old favorites from Cafe Brenda.

I believe passionately in the need to augment our diets with whole grains, beans, fruits, and vegetables while reducing our intake of meats and foods laden with salts, sugars, and trans fats. I am striving to make people aware that a good diet is one that is truly balanced, personal, and doable, and that a diet rich in plant-based proteins is the best insurance policy against many of the illnesses plaguing our nation. *The Spoonriver Cookbook* has been written with care and love to inspire the most timid as well as the most experienced cook, and I hope it will serve as a guide to the good life, and a guide to a long life.

Take this book into your kitchen and have fun, teach your kids to cook, make healthy meals the heart of your day, share the bounty of the land. Who knows, one of these recipes may prompt your own "boiled dinner" moment and send you on a path to wellness that you never imagined. Nothing could make me happier!

MILL CITY FARMERS MARKET //

THE MILL CITY FARMERS MARKET was founded in June 2006 by Brenda Langton, in collaboration with the Minnesota Historical Society's Mill City Museum, to promote healthy foods and local farmers. Its mission is to promote local, sustainable, and organic agriculture and increase economic opportunities for farmers, urban youth, small businesses, and food artisans. It also seeks to offer experiential learning about and access to healthy local foods and build a vibrant gathering place for Minneapolis residents and visitors.

Located in downtown Minneapolis on the Chicago Mall between the Guthrie Theater and Spoonriver and in the historic train shed of the Mill City Museum (built in the ruins of the Washburn A Mill), the Mill City Farmers Market overlooks the historic Stone Arch Bridge and the Mississippi River. The market brings together farmers, producers, food artisans, multicultural food traditions, celebrity chefs, authors, cooking demos, free food samples, recipes, kids' activities, farm animals, contests, festivals, and live music to educate consumers about sustainable and organic agriculture and our regional farmers. The market builds connections and fosters relationships between farmers, entrepreneurs, and customers in a fun and lively environment. Preference is given to growers and

The Mill City Farmers Market is partially housed in the train shed of the old Washburn A Mill.

vendors who use sustainable practices in producing and manufacturing their goods. Organic certification is not required, though it is respected and encouraged.

Herb grower John Bennett of Bennett's Farm

The Mill City Farmers Market is a beautiful outdoor shopping experience enjoyed each market day by more than five thousand guests from all over Minnesota as well as national and international tourists. A vital part of the downtown community, the Mill City Farmers Market is a valuable and cherished amenity for our downtown neighbors and one of the most distinctive markets in the Midwest.

Throughout this cookbook you will see photographs by Mette Nielsen that feature the market experience and many of the wonderful vendors who also grow for Spoonriver. Please visit millcityfarmersmarket.org for the latest information on what's going on at the market.

appetizers

Radish and Herb Butter Canapés

Simple, beautiful, and delicious. Why do so many people avoid radishes? They have many health benefits and are a sure sign of spring. There are as many variations to this recipe as there are types of butter and bread. // **MAKES 10 TO 12 CANAPÉS**

2 tablespoons chopped fresh chives or parsley
4 tablespoons butter, softened
1 bunch red, Easter, or French breakfast radishes

Thinly sliced multigrain bread, cut into bite-size pieces
Sea salt

Fold the chopped herbs into the softened butter.

Wash and thinly slice the radishes. Put them in a bowl of cold water.

Spread approximately ¼ to ½ teaspoon of butter onto a piece of bread and top it with a radish slice or two. Just before serving, sprinkle with a little sea salt.

Variation

Omit the fresh herbs and add a little wasabi, white miso, or umeboshi plum to the butter.

Sesame Butter and Miso Pâté

This pâté has been a mainstay on our appetizer menu for many years. It is definitely one of our most requested recipes. Serve it with a large assortment of fresh vegetables and crackers. This is a great choice for large crowds: it's healthy, delicious, and easy to make. I love it on toast in the morning with a little mustard and lettuce or sprouts. Tahini, a great source of vitamin E, is available raw or roasted. This recipe calls for roasted tahini, which is made with roasted sesame seeds. // **MAKES 2 CUPS**

1½ cups roasted (not raw) tahini
1 teaspoon garlic salt or 1 clove garlic, crushed
½ tablespoon dried basil
4 tablespoons red or yellow miso
    (not dark brown miso)

½ to ¾ cup water
1½ tablespoons chopped fresh parsley
2 tablespoons chopped green onions (optional)

Combine the tahini, garlic, basil, and miso in a food processor or mixer. (An electric mixer or food processor will give you the best texture, but you can get a good result mixing by hand with a sturdy whisk or wooden spoon.) If using fresh garlic, add a little salt. Mix well.

Add the water ¼ cup at a time, combining well after each addition. Roasted tahini varies in thickness, so if your tahini is very thick, use more water as needed to get a creamy, spreadable texture. If the mixture separates, add more water and keep stirring. It will come together like a creamy peanut butter.

Stir in the parsley and green onions.

Hummus

Hummus is very easy to make and often much better than the prepared hummus in the grocery store, which can be old and overpowering with garlic and cumin. For a spicier version, you can easily add more garlic and some hot pepper. If you are a fan of preserved lemons, we swear by adding them to our hummus. Another nice option is to roast the garlic; however, we still like a little raw garlic as well. Serve hummus with raw vegetables and whole wheat bread or pita bread and olives. // **MAKES 2 CUPS**

1 (15-ounce) can chickpeas, drained
2 medium cloves garlic
1 tablespoon lemon juice
3 tablespoons olive oil

3 tablespoons tahini
½ teaspoon salt
¼ cup water
1 tablespoon parsley, chopped

Put all of the ingredients in a food processor or blender and puree until smooth.

Variation

To add preserved lemon, use 1 tablespoon of chopped rind. You may want to cut back on the lemon juice. Taste and add more lemon if needed.

Roasted Sweet Pepper, Walnut, and Pomegranate Spread

This rich and very zippy dip dances on your tongue. The ingredient that makes it so dynamic is pomegranate molasses from Lebanon. If you don't own a bottle, trust me, you will be happy once you track one down. We serve this spread with our creamy hummus, which is a perfect complement. Vegetables, olives, and focaccia, pita, or your favorite bread all go beautifully on a platter with this spread. Substituting flaxseed for the bread crumbs makes this wheat free. // **MAKES 1½ CUPS**

2 large red bell peppers or canned, roasted red peppers
1 cup walnuts
3 tablespoons bread crumbs or ground flaxseed
1 tablespoon pomegranate molasses
1 tablespoon lemon juice

½ teaspoon salt
½ teaspoon cumin
1 teaspoon minced fresh garlic
1 tablespoon water
2 to 3 tablespoons olive oil

If you use canned, roasted peppers, choose those packed in juice or water rather than vinegar.

Preheat the oven to 425 degrees. Rub the peppers lightly with oil, and place them in the oven until the skins blister and lightly brown, about 30 minutes. Turn them with a tong once or twice. You can also roast them over an open flame, turning them until all sides are evenly charred.

Place the peppers in a paper bag or in a covered bowl so the peppers sweat. Sweating the peppers makes them steam a little, which makes it easier to peel them. When they are cool enough to handle, peel the peppers.

Roast the walnuts for about 12 minutes at 350 degrees. Try to rub off some of their skins once the nuts are roasted. The skins can dull the color of the dip.

While the peppers are sweating, mix the bread crumbs, molasses, lemon juice, salt, cumin, garlic, water, and olive oil together. Let the mixture sit for 5 minutes to soften the bread crumbs.

Place the peppers and the bread crumb mixture in a food processor and pulse until everything is in small pieces but the spread still has some texture to it.

Add the walnuts and carefully pulse until the walnuts are small but still have some texture. This step is very important, so take it slow. This dish comes together when all the pieces are small, but you still have pieces of walnut to bite into.

Hummus and Roasted Sweet Pepper, Walnut, and Pomegranate Spread

White Bean and Sun-Dried Tomato Dip

This is a type of Tuscan hummus. It is delicious with vegetables and crackers and can even make a nice sandwich spread. // **MAKES 2 CUPS**

⅓ cup sun-dried tomatoes
1 (15-ounce) can cannellini beans, drained and rinsed
2 teaspoons white miso (optional)
2 teaspoons minced garlic

1 teaspoon fresh lemon juice
1 teaspoon salt
2 tablespoons olive oil
1½ teaspoons chopped fresh rosemary

Place the tomatoes in a small bowl and cover them with warm water. Let them sit until the tomatoes are plump. Drain the tomatoes and then dice them.

Combine the beans, miso, garlic, lemon juice, salt, and olive oil in a food processor or blender. Puree.

Place the bean mixture in a bowl and fold in the tomatoes and rosemary.

Adjust the seasoning to taste, perhaps adding more garlic or rosemary.

Serve on crackers or toasted French bread.

Yogurt Herb Dip

This recipe originates from an Afghani chutney that my friend Zaytoona used to make for us to dip flat bread in at dinner. We like it for a vegetable dip or as a lively complement to a simple meal of rice, beans, and vegetables. It is very fresh and easy to make. **|| MAKES 2 CUPS**

1 bunch cilantro (about 3 cups lightly packed), rinsed
1 bunch mint (1½ to 2 cups), stemmed and rinsed well
2 teaspoons minced garlic
1 teaspoon salt

2 teaspoons lemon juice (optional)
1 teaspoon honey (optional)
12 ounces plain yogurt

Finely chop the herbs and combine them in a bowl with the garlic and salt. Add the lemon juice and honey (if using). Gently whisk in the yogurt.

Roasted Eggplant Salsa

This is a great salsa for pita chips, or use it in a quesadilla. It is also delicious on broiled fish or chicken.

// **MAKES 6 TO 8 SERVINGS**

2 medium eggplants
1 red bell pepper
1 green bell pepper
1 bunch green onions, sliced
1 large tomato, diced
3 large cloves garlic, minced

Juice of 1 lemon
Juice of 1 small lime
⅓ cup olive oil
2 tablespoons chopped cilantro
Salt
Jalapeño, seeded and chopped (optional)

Slowly roast the eggplants on top of the stove over a medium-low open flame. Turn the eggplant as it chars. Once the whole eggplant is charred and soft, carefully scrape off the charred skin. Chop the eggplant flesh.

Roast the bell peppers in a 425-degree oven or on top of the stove, like the eggplant. Place the roasted peppers in a paper bag and close it to sweat the peppers. Once the peppers have cooled enough to handle, peel and dice them.

Combine all the ingredients in a bowl. Add salt to taste.

Mill City Farmers Market vendors Noryeng and Che Chang

Baba Ghanoush

Picking out eggplant to take home can be tricky. It is important to make sure that it is fresh with no soft spots. The creamy white flesh of a roasted eggplant makes this dip especially lovely with pita bread and some salty olives and refreshing cucumbers. This recipe has the right balance of nutty tahini (which is simply ground raw sesame seeds), lemon, garlic, and olive oil.

Tahini varies in thickness, so be prepared to adjust the recipe a little by adding more liquid to get the consistency you want. The oil in tahini often rises to the top of the container. Stir it well before using. A trick for storing tahini is to turn the container upside down now and again so it remains mixed. // **MAKES 1½ TO 2 CUPS**

1 medium-large eggplant
3 tablespoons tahini
2 tablespoons lemon juice
2 to 4 cloves garlic, chopped
3 tablespoons olive oil
Salt
2 tablespoons chopped fresh parsley

Roast the eggplant. We like to roast the eggplant over the flames of a burner on top of a gas range. Place the eggplant on the grate and turn it occasionally until the eggplant is charred on all sides. This must be done over medium-low heat. Be gentle turning the eggplant so it doesn't get punctured and lose its juices—and mess up your stove. This is a fragrant experience but gives the eggplant a nice smoky flavor.

Heirloom eggplant varieties originally native to Thailand, India, China, Africa, Japan, and Italy, among other countries, also grow well in the Upper Midwest.

You can also roast the eggplant whole in the oven, but you won't get the same smoky flavor. Preheat the oven to 350 degrees. Lightly oil the outside of the eggplant. Place it on a cookie sheet and put in the oven. Turn the eggplant after 15 minutes and continue roasting until it is soft and wrinkled. Let the eggplant cool. When it is cool enough to handle, peel the skin off.

Combine the eggplant pulp with the tahini, lemon juice, garlic, and 2 tablespoons of the olive oil in a food processor. Blend together until smooth. Taste. Add salt and more garlic or lemon to taste. Quantities will vary with this recipe, depending on the size of the eggplant, the thickness of the tahini, and the pungency of the garlic.

Stir in the chopped parsley. Place the baba ghanoush in a bowl. Just before serving, drizzle with the remaining tablespoon of olive oil.

Serve with pita bread and vegetables.

Caponata

This is a good dish to make a day ahead of time to allow the savory and sweet flavors some time to meld. We like to leave the skin on the eggplant for its beautiful purple color. Serve with crostini spread with a mild goat cheese, then topped with caponata. **|| MAKES ABOUT 6 CUPS**

1 medium eggplant
⅓ cup olive oil
3 stalks celery, diced small
1 large onion, diced small
1 tablespoon minced garlic
½ cup green olives, coarsely chopped
1½ tablespoons capers

½ cup golden raisins
2 tablespoons chopped parsley
2 tablespoons red wine vinegar
6 tablespoons tomato paste, dissolved in ⅔ cup water
Honey to taste (about 2 teaspoons)
Salt and pepper

Wash the eggplant and cut it into ½-inch slices, leaving the skin on. Sprinkle the slices with salt and let them sit for 30 minutes until the eggplant sweats out its bitter juices. (The fresher the eggplant, the less likely it will be bitter. If you have beautiful, fresh eggplant and you want to skip this step, feel free to.) Rinse the eggplant and pat it dry. Cut the slices into ½-inch cubes.

In a heavy skillet, heat the olive oil and sauté the celery, onion, and garlic over low heat for about 5 minutes.

Add the eggplant and sauté about 10 more minutes.

Add the olives, capers, raisins, parsley, vinegar, tomato paste, and honey. Simmer for about 15 minutes, or until the juices are gone. Season with salt and pepper.

Sunflower Pesto

This is a nice sandwich spread. Or serve it on French bread or as a dip for vegetables.

// MAKES 4 CUPS

1 cup basil leaves, coarsely chopped
½ cup parsley, coarsely chopped
½ cake soft tofu
½ cup olive oil
1 tablespoon chopped garlic
½ bunch green onions, chopped into 1-inch pieces
 2 tablespoons fresh lemon juice
1½ tablespoons Dijon mustard
1 teaspoon salt
1¼ teaspoons pepper
½ cup water
1 cup raw unsalted sunflower seeds, toasted; or roasted
    unsalted sunflower seeds

Place everything except the water and the sunflower seeds in a food processor and chop until medium fine.

Add the water and sunflower seeds, and pulse until the mixture is creamy but slightly chunky in texture.

Great bunches of basil begin to appear in the market at midsummer.

Black Olive–Walnut Tapenade

This recipe calls for Moroccan olives, which we really like in a tapenade; however, you can make this tapenade with kalamatas or another good black olive. Soak the olives if they are salty. The variation, made with tofu, makes a great spread or dip. // **MAKES 1½ CUPS**

1 cup pitted Moroccan olives, rinsed well
2 cloves garlic, coarsely chopped
⅓ cup chopped walnuts
3 tablespoons olive oil
3 tablespoons minced green onions or 2 tablespoons
    chopped red onion

3 tablespoons chopped fresh basil
1 tablespoon fresh lemon juice
3 tablespoons water
Pepper

In a food processor, chop up the olives, garlic, and walnuts. Drizzle in the olive oil. Do not overprocess, you want to retain some texture.

Stir in the green onion, basil, lemon juice, water, and pepper.

Variation

Okay, we know this sounds a little weird, but this tapenade is really good when you add half a cake of pureed tofu. It turns the tapenade into a great sandwich spread or a less salty dip for vegetables and pita.

Transfer the tapenade to a bowl. Place 6 ounces of firm or extra-firm tofu in the food processor (no need to rinse it since you'll later mix the tofu with the tapenade). Puree until smooth; then fold into the tapenade.

Warmed Spiced Olives

Spiced olives are a great addition to an appetizer plate. They can also be served with couscous and roasted vegetables or with hummus and pita bread. When buying olives, seek out a good source that carries a variety of quality olives, such as specialty delis and cheese shops. When choosing olives from a grocery store's olive bar, trust your nose more than anything to ensure that you are getting the freshest olives possible. Generally speaking, buy olives with pits, although for cooking it can be more convenient to buy pitted. // MAKES 3 CUPS

1 to 2 tablespoons olive oil
2 cloves garlic, chopped
½ tablespoon whole coriander seeds

2 teaspoons fennel seeds
3 cups kalamata or assorted olives
Lemon zest or dried chili flakes (optional)

Heat the olive oil in a sauté pan large enough to fit the olives. Add the garlic and sauté over medium heat for just a minute.

Add the coriander and fennel seeds to toast for just another minute. Do not let the garlic brown. You may need to turn down the heat.

Reduce the heat to low, add the olives, and cook until the olives are warmed.

Serve warm or at room temperature.

Note: If the olives are very salty, soak them in water for ½ hour. Drain and rinse well. Olives will last in the fridge for 2 to 3 weeks.

Warmed Spiced Olives

Green Olive Tapenade

This tapenade can be made with any flavorful pitted green olive. Or you can pit the olives yourself by smashing them with the bottom of a cup and then pulling out the pit. To save time, first smash all the olives and then pull out the pits. Rinse them to remove some of the salt. Serve the tapenade with crackers or bread. Tapenade is also tasty on pasta or spread on broiled chicken or fish. **// MAKES 1½ CUPS**

5 medium cloves garlic, chopped
3 tablespoons olive oil
1 cup pitted green olives
½ cup parsley, washed and chopped

2 tablespoons finely chopped red onion
1 tablespoons lemon juice
Freshly ground pepper
½ cake firm tofu (optional)

Sauté the garlic in the olive oil until it is lightly browned (be careful not burn it); then allow it to cool slightly.

Combine all of the ingredients in a food processor. Pulse until the particles are nice and small, but do not overdo it.

If you are adding tofu, transfer the tapenade to a bowl. Place the tofu in the food processor (no need to rinse it since you'll later mix the tofu with the tapenade). Puree until smooth and then fold into the tapenade.

Shrimp Quesadillas with Coconut Cilantro Salsa

This recipe is a great way to use the massive bunches of mint and cilantro you get all summer at your farmers' market. The salsa is really more of an East Indian chutney and was a favorite at Cafe Brenda for years. It's so fresh and lively, it will snap your taste buds from Oaxaca to Mumbai. We serve it at the restaurant with chopped cooked shrimp. // **MAKES 2 CUPS OF SALSA AND 4 QUESADILLAS**

COCONUT CILANTRO SALSA //

½ cup coarsely chopped cilantro

2 tablespoons coarsely chopped fresh mint

2 tablespoons coarsely chopped jalapeño

¾ cup unsweetened shredded coconut

½ cup light coconut milk

⅓ cup lime juice

1 tablespoon honey

½ teaspoon salt

¼ teaspoon pepper

⅓ cup water

To make the salsa, coarsely chop the cilantro, mint, and jalapeños in a food processor. Add the coconut, coconut milk, lime juice, honey, salt, and pepper. Pulse just until combined. Add water as needed, making sure that the salsa is not too thin.

Assemble the quesadillas by spreading 4 tortillas with about 3 tablespoons of salsa verde each. Then add a layer of the cheese and 2 to 3 tablespoons of chopped shrimp or chicken to each. Top each quesadilla with another tortilla.

SHRIMP QUESADILLAS //

8 (6- or 8-inch) flour tortillas

1 (12-ounce) jar mild or medium salsa verde (tomatillo-based salsa)

½ pound jack or cheddar cheese, coarsely grated

¾ to 1 pound cooked shrimp or chicken, chopped

Olive or vegetable oil

Heat a little oil in a large skillet or cast-iron pan. Cook the quesadillas until they are lightly browned and crisp. You can also cook them on a cookie sheet in a 350-degree oven. Turn after 3 or 4 minutes to brown both sides.

Serve topped with coconut cilantro salsa.

Smoked Salmon Quesadillas

Quesadillas are a good appetizer for parties. You can make them up ahead of time, and then heating them up during a party is a snap. For a meal, simply add a green salad. **// MAKES 6 QUESADILLAS**

1 bunch green onions or chives
12 (6- to 8-inch) flour tortillas
¾ to 1 cup sour cream

Chopped dill, tarragon, or basil (optional)
8 ounces cold smoked salmon, thinly sliced
Olive or vegetable oil

Wash the green onions and remove the roots. Chop the green onions, including the greens.

Spread 6 tortillas with a generous 2 tablespoons of the sour cream each. Sprinkle the green onions and herbs on top; then add the salmon slices.

Place a second tortilla on the top of each prepared tortilla. Brush the top tortilla with olive or vegetable oil. Turn the quesadillas over to brush the bottom tortilla with oil.

There are two options for cooking the quesadillas. You can cook them on top of the stove in a skillet over medium heat, or place them on a cookie sheet in a preheated 350-degree oven. Turn the quesadillas after 3 or 4 minutes and continue to bake for another 3 or 4 minutes. The tortillas will be golden brown and the insides heated through.

Slice the quesadillas into wedges and serve them with salsa. Our mango salsa (page 165) is really good with these!

Smoked Salmon Quesadillas

Butternut Squash–Chipotle Quesadillas

Butternut squash paired with spicy chipotle pepper makes a delicious combination of sweet and smoky flavors. Smoked paprika and chili powder are not quite as hot and may be more likely to be in your spice drawer than chipotle powder. Both are good options. Serve the quesadillas with your favorite salsa as an appetizer or with bean soup or chili for a complete meal. **|| MAKES 6 QUESADILLAS**

Butternut squash, harvested, cured, and headed to the market

1 butternut squash or 2 cups frozen squash or
    canned pumpkin
1 cup chopped leeks or onion
1 tablespoon vegetable oil or olive oil
1 teaspoon chopped garlic
Salt
Pepper
2 cups grated white cheddar cheese
1 teaspoon ground chipotle powder
12 (8-inch) flour tortillas

If using fresh squash, cut it in half, scoop out the seeds, and bake it on a cookie sheet at 350 degrees until soft, approximately 45 minutes. Scoop out the flesh and mash it well. Measure out 2 cups of mashed squash, and freeze the rest for another use.

Sauté the leeks in the oil for 3 to 4 minutes. Add the garlic and cook another minute. Add salt and pepper to taste. Add the leek mixture to the squash and let it cool.

In another bowl, combine the grated cheese and chipotle powder.

Preheat the oven to 400 degrees. Place 3 tortillas each on 2 lightly oiled cookie sheets. Divide the filling evenly among the 6 tortillas, spreading it to the edge. Distribute the cheese over the squash filling, and place the remaining tortillas on top. Lightly brush the top tortilla with oil.

Bake for approximately 8 minutes, or until golden brown. Slice the quesadillas into quarters to serve. You can also cook these over medium heat in a frying pan brushed with oil.

soups

Vegetable Stock

Making stock does not take much time. It can be simmering while you are preparing the soup vegetables; it can also be made ahead of time and refrigerated or frozen until you are ready for it. Some soups can be made with water instead of stock, but stock always adds to the flavor. We do not have one all-purpose stock recipe: our stock varies with the kind of soup we are making and what we have on hand.

*There are certain vegetables that are basic to every stock: onion, celery, carrots, and herbs. Our recipe includes these and more, along with some suggestions for variations. Some of our soup recipes list specific stock additions; other recipes simply call for vegetable stock. Use this basic recipe, adjusting it to fit what you have on hand in your kitchen. // **MAKES 6 TO 8 CUPS***

1 tablespoon vegetable oil
1 medium onion, chopped
2 carrots, chopped
2 stalks celery, chopped (celery leaves are nice too)
6 to 8 cups water

2 to 3 cloves garlic, smashed
6 to 8 sprigs fresh parsley
Fresh or dried herbs, such as bay leaves, thyme,
    and marjoram
Peppercorns

Heat the vegetable oil in a soup pot and sauté the onions, carrots, and celery until lightly browned, about 5 to 7 minutes. When you sauté the vegetables, you help bring out their flavors. (Skip this step if you want to reduce the stock's fat content and make a lighter stock.)

Add the water, garlic, parsley sprigs, herbs, and peppercorns to the soup pot and bring the water to a boil.

Reduce the heat and simmer for 20 to 30 minutes. Remove from the heat and strain. Do not let unstrained stock sit: some vegetables may turn the stock bitter if they sit for any length of time.

Optional Ingredients for Stock Making

Winter squash The peels and seeds of winter squash add a lot of flavor and body to stock. They are especially good in soups containing winter squash. Cut up the squash for your soup before you make the stock and use the peels and seeds in your stock.

Summer squash Stock is a good use for summer squash when you have mountains of it from the garden. It adds a delicate flavor, a nice addition to summer soups.

Parsnip If you have unwaxed parsnips from the market or your garden, use the peelings and cores for a slightly sweet flavor.

Broccoli stems Peel and save the broccoli stems. Chop them and add them to the stock for an earthy taste.

Leeks Use leeks instead of, or in addition to, onions. Leeks are milder and sweeter than onions. Some recipes calling for leeks ask for the bulbous white end only. Save the leaves for soup stock. 1 cup of chopped leaves is enough for 6 cups of stock.

Mushrooms Wild mushrooms, although expensive, add a tremendous amount of flavor. Just a few stems or broken pieces will go a long way. Dried mushrooms, shiitake, porcini, and morels all have unique, woodsy flavors. Add them to any stock being used in stews and soups that contain mushrooms. Domestic button mushrooms will be delicious too.

Green beans We always seem to have some tough, overgrown beans that are not suitable for serving. These add a lot of flavor to summer stocks.

Corn cobs After slicing the corn from the cobs for the corn chowder recipe, you'll have cobs full of sweet corn milk. Add these cobs to the stockpot for a great corn flavor. Corn cobs may be used in stock for other soups as well; just remember that they result in a slightly milky liquid that you may not want to use for a clear soup.

Bonito fish flakes Bonito flakes add a mild, smoky fish flavor to stock. They are often used in Asian cooking. Add a small amount to stock for a fuller flavor.

Melon Mint Soup

There is nothing like the taste sensation of a really good cantaloupe or honeydew. When melon is at its peak, everyone at the market is searching for the perfect melon. As we all know, it's a real bummer to come home with a bland one. Choose a melon that has an aroma and is slightly soft at the bottom. This soup blends that wonderful melon flavor with a hint of mint, a great combination. This is a good first course for a summer brunch. // **SERVES 4 TO 6**

1 large (about 3 pounds) cantaloupe
½ cup apple juice
1½ tablespoons lime juice
1½ tablespoons chopped fresh mint

½ cup plain yogurt
1 tablespoon honey, if needed
Pinch of salt

Cut the melon into chunks, reserving the juices. Put the melon and its juice in a blender along with the apple juice and lime juice, and blend until smooth. Add the mint for just a few seconds at the end.

Pour the soup into a bowl and whisk in the yogurt. Taste the soup and correct the seasonings. You may want to add more mint or perhaps a little honey.

Cold Split Pea Soup with Mint

This is a filling cold soup. Served with bread and fruit or salad, it makes a complete meal for the hot summer months. When the soup is pureed, it has a wonderful creamy texture. Top it with croutons.
*// **SERVES 6 TO 8***

1½ cups green split peas
4 cups water or vegetable stock
1 small onion, sliced
2 cloves garlic, crushed

2 (3-inch) sprigs fresh mint
Salt
2 cups plain yogurt or 1 cup yogurt and 1 cup sour cream

Rinse the peas well and put them in a pot with about 4 cups of lightly salted water. Bring the water to a boil and let the peas boil for 5 minutes. Remove from the heat and drain.

Put the peas back in the saucepan with 4 cups of water or vegetable stock. Bring to a boil and add the onion, garlic, mint, and salt. Reduce the heat and simmer until the peas are tender, approximately 45 minutes.

Discard the mint and puree the peas in a blender, working in small batches to prevent an explosion of hot liquid. Cool the soup thoroughly (this will take about 4 hours).

Before serving, whisk in the yogurt. Garnish each bowl with a dollop of yogurt or sour cream and a sprig of mint.

Gazpacho

Gazpacho is a cold mixed-vegetable soup. There are many variations—some blended, some made with chunks of bread. Use what you have at hand. Add more garlic or hot peppers to suit your taste. Chop, grate, and dice vegetables as appropriate to create a nice mix of textures. // **MAKES 6 CUPS**

4 large whole tomatoes
1 small cucumber
1 red bell pepper
¾ cup shredded carrot
½ cup thinly sliced celery
¼ cup chopped sweet onion
2 large cloves garlic, finely chopped
1 teaspoon salt
2 tablespoons chopped fresh basil
⅛ teaspoon cayenne
1 fresh jalapeño (optional)
2 tablespoons olive oil
2 tablespoons lemon or lime juice
½ cup parsley, coarsely chopped

Peel and seed the tomatoes, saving the juice in a bowl. To peel tomatoes, cut a small x in the blossom (non-stem) end. Drop them into boiling water until the skin begins to loosen, usually less than 30 seconds. Rinse the tomatoes under cold water to stop the cooking, and remove the peels with a paring knife. To seed a tomato, cut a wedge around the core and remove it; then cut the tomato in half. Squeeze out the seeds into a bowl. Strain and reserve the juice. Dice three tomatoes, and juice the fourth. (You'll need about 1 cup of tomato juice. You can supplement with canned tomato juice if necessary.) Place the diced tomatoes in a large bowl.

Ah, tomato season!

Peel and seed the cucumber. Dice it and add it to the bowl with the tomatoes.

Dice the bell pepper. Add it to the tomatoes and cucumbers along with the carrot, celery, and onion. Add the garlic, salt, and basil. Stir well. Add the cayenne and jalapeño, if using. Add the olive oil, lemon juice, parsley, and reserved tomato juice. Stir well. Taste and adjust the seasoning as needed.

Serve the soup cold or at room temperature. Garnish with croutons and black olives.

Cucumber Dill Soup

This soup is very refreshing. It is great for a hot summer day and is a good way to use up the abundance of cucumbers in season. Stay away from the big cukes, because they can impart a bitter taste to the soup.
// SERVES 4 TO 6

4 medium cucumbers, peeled, seeded, and chopped
4 green onions, chopped
1 tablespoon butter or olive oil
Salt
Pepper

2 teaspoons chopped fresh dill or 1 teaspoon dried
1 cup vegetable stock or water
¾ cup plain yogurt
Sour cream

Sauté the cucumbers and green onions in butter until the cucumber is tender.

Add salt and pepper to taste; then puree the cucumber mixture in a blender with the dill and stock. Allow the soup to cool. Combine it with the yogurt and adjust the seasonings. Chill well.

Garnish the soup with fresh dill, green onions, and sour cream.

Asparagus Soup

For those of us in northern climates, asparagus is one of the first fresh vegetables we enjoy in the spring. Potato and zucchini help give this dish a perfect consistency without a traditional roux of flour and butter, making it a healthier dish.

// SERVES 4 TO 6

1½ pounds asparagus
1 tablespoon olive oil
1 leek or small onion, sliced
1 large potato, peeled and diced large
3 cups chopped zucchini
4 cups vegetable stock
Salt
Pepper

Peel the asparagus. Cut off and save the tips. Cut the stalks into 1- to 2-inch pieces and set them aside. Bring some water to a boil in a small pan, add the asparagus tips, reduce the heat, and simmer until done. Drain and set aside.

Heat the olive oil in a soup pot and sauté the leek for a few minutes. Add the potato, zucchini, and asparagus stalks and continue to sauté a few more minutes. Add the stock, bring it to a boil, and then reduce the heat and simmer, covered, for approximately 15 minutes.

Get it while you can—asparagus season is fleeting in the Midwest.

Puree the soup, working in small batches to prevent an explosion of hot liquid, and return it to the soup pot. Add the asparagus tips and season with salt and pepper. Heat for a few minutes and serve.

Beet Borscht

We love the sweet flavor and brilliant red color of beets. Using frozen orange juice concentrate will give you a more intense orange flavor, but you can substitute the juice of an orange or a half cup of orange juice. This is a hearty soup that, served with bread and cheese, is a full meal. // **SERVES 6 TO 8**

SOUPS

1 tablespoon vegetable oil
1 cup chopped onion
1 carrot, peeled and sliced
1 stalk celery, chopped
1 cup chopped green cabbage
2 large beets, peeled and cut into large chunks
1 potato, cut into chunks

1 teaspoon caraway seeds
5 cups vegetable stock
1 teaspoon salt
1 tablespoon cider vinegar or white wine vinegar
1 tablespoon frozen orange juice concentrate
   or juice of 1 orange
1 cup chopped tomato (optional)

Heat the oil in a soup pot. Sauté the onion until it's soft. Add the carrots, celery, and cabbage. Continue sautéing, stirring, over medium heat for 5 minutes. Add the beets, potatoes, and caraway seeds.

Add the stock and salt. Bring it to a boil; then turn down the heat and simmer for 15 to 20 minutes, until the potatoes and beets are tender.

Add the vinegar and orange juice. If using the tomato, add it now. Simmer on low heat for 10 minutes.

Serve the borscht warm with a dollop of sour cream and a sprinkle of fresh chopped dill.

Midseason bounty

Carrot Soup

You can also make this soup with some parsnips or sweet potatoes; simply substitute them for up to one-half of the carrots. // **SERVES 4 TO 6**

2 tablespoons vegetable oil
1 leek (white part only) or onion, chopped
7 to 8 large carrots, sliced (6 cups)
1 teaspoon chopped fresh thyme or ½ teaspoon dried

1 teaspoon salt
4 cups vegetable stock
Crème fraîche or chopped olives, for garnish

Heat the oil in a large saucepan. Sauté the leek until tender. Add the carrot slices. Cook, stirring often, for 5 minutes. You want the carrots to brown a little.

Add the thyme and salt, and then add the stock and bring it to a boil. Turn down the heat and simmer for 20 to 30 minutes, until the carrots are tender.

Puree the soup, working in small batches to prevent an explosion of hot liquid, until it is smooth.

Garnish the soup with crème fraîche or chopped chives.

Roasted Tomato Soup

When they are available, make this soup with fresh garden tomatoes. The rest of the year, use canned roasted tomatoes. Serve the soup with a loaf of fresh baked bread or grilled cheese sandwiches.

// SERVES 4

1 medium onion, chopped
1 tablespoon olive oil
1 stalk celery, chopped
3 cups roasted and chopped fresh tomatoes or
    1 (28-ounce) can roasted diced tomatoes

1 cup vegetable stock or water
1 to 2 tablespoons chopped fresh basil
½ teaspoon salt
Pepper

Sauté the onion in olive oil until it's translucent. Add the celery and sauté until it is tender, about 5 minutes.

Set aside ½ cup of the diced tomato, and combine the rest of the tomatoes with the onion mixture, stock, basil, salt, and pepper in a soup pot. Simmer for 10 minutes.

Puree the soup in a blender until it is smooth. Stir the reserved tomatoes into the soup.

For a creamy soup, add ½ cup of half-and-half or heavy cream.

ROASTING FRESH TOMATOES //

You can roast tomatoes under a broiler or on a grill. If using a grill, make sure the tomatoes are firm, even a little under ripe, so they do not fall apart.

Set the oven rack at least 5 inches from the broiler. Cut the tomatoes in half and remove the seeds. Rub the tomato halves with olive oil and sprinkle them with salt and pepper. Place them in a broiling pan or on a sided sheet pan cut-side up.

You do not need to turn the tomatoes once they are in the oven. Broil until the tomatoes begin to shrivel and soften.

To roast tomatoes on the grill, place them directly on the grill grate cut-side down. Grill until lightly charred, just a few minutes, and then turn them and continue grilling until they are softened, about 10 minutes total.

Ginger Squash Soup

This rich and creamy soup is often requested in fall and winter. We consider it to be the ultimate comfort food. You can experiment with the many winter squash varieties. Some are sweeter or richer than others, but they all make great soup.

// SERVES 4 TO 6

1 medium butternut or buttercup squash
2 tablespoons vegetable oil or butter
1 medium yellow onion, chopped
3 tablespoons peeled and chopped ginger root
2 large cloves garlic, chopped
4 cups vegetable stock or water
3 tablespoons yellow or white miso (optional)
½ teaspoon salt
¼ teaspoon white pepper
Juice of 1 orange
¼ to ½ cup half-and-half (optional)

Wash the squash well and peel it. Save the peelings to use for making stock (see page 24).

Chop the squash into 1-inch pieces, discarding the seeds. You should have about 4½ cups of chopped squash.

Heat the oil in a large soup pot, and sauté the onion, ginger, and garlic. When the onion has softened, add the squash.

Assorted winter squash, including butternut, kabocha, acorn, delicata, and carnival

Add the stock and cover the pot. Simmer over medium heat for 30 to 40 minutes. Add the miso (if using), salt, pepper, and orange juice.

Working in small batches, puree the soup in a blender until smooth. Stir in the half-and-half (if using). If the soup is too thick, add more stock.

Corn Chowder

Because there are now so many corn hybrids that extend the growing season—some ripen in early summer and some in late fall—we have the opportunity to make fresh corn chowder more often than in the past. Nothing can equal the sweet, rich flavor of the "milk" from fresh corn cobs. Our version of corn chowder has no cream, but is plenty rich without it. When fresh corn is not available, use frozen. You can use frozen corn on the cob, although it is a little harder to handle when scraping the cobs. You can also use a bag of frozen corn. The soup will not be as creamy, but it will still taste great. // **SERVES 6 TO 8**

8 ears fresh or frozen sweet corn or 1 (16-ounce)
    bag frozen corn kernels
1 medium onion, chopped
2 tablespoons vegetable oil or butter
2 medium carrots, diced
2 stalks celery, diced
3 medium potatoes, cubed (3 cups)

5 cups vegetable stock made with scraped corn cobs
    (see page 24)
1 teaspoon salt, or to taste
1 to 2 teaspoons fresh herbs, such as thyme, parsley,
    or basil
Freshly ground pepper

Use two methods to remove kernels from the cob so you will have two different textures. Cut the kernels from four of the ears. Starting at the tip of each ear, cut straight down, removing the kernels but leaving about ⅛ inch of pulp on the cob.

Scrape the kernels from the remaining four ears. With a sharp knife, slice through the center of a row of kernels from the tip to the end of the ear. Repeat until you have sliced open every row. Lay the ear over a bowl and scrape the kernels with a knife, pushing the milk from the corn. Work your way around the whole ear, extracting as much of the milk as you can. Combine the cut and scraped kernels in a bowl and set it aside. Use the cobs to make your stock.

Sauté the onion in the oil for 3 to 5 minutes. Add the carrots and celery and sauté another 5 to 8 minutes, until the vegetables are soft.

Add the potatoes, corn, and stock. Season with the salt, herbs, and freshly ground pepper to taste. Simmer for 20 minutes.

Remove 2 cups of the soup, puree it in a blender, and return it to the pot. The soup is now ready to serve or may be kept at a low simmer until ready to serve.

Golden Potage

This assortment of sweet root vegetables produces a very rustic, comforting soup. No single vegetable dominates, resulting in a delicate flavor. We like to make this in the fall and early winter, when root vegetables are freshest and at their sweetest. // **SERVES 6**

3 tablespoons butter
1 cup chopped leek or sweet onion
8 cloves garlic, chopped
1 to 1½ cups diced sweet potato or winter squash
½ cup chopped parsnip or rutabaga
½ cup chopped carrot

1½ cups diced potato
4 cups vegetable stock
1 teaspoon salt
½ cup half-and-half, milk, or grain milk
1 tablespoon chopped fresh herbs, such as thyme or
    marjoram, or 1 teaspoon dried

Melt the butter in a soup pot and sauté the leek and garlic for 5 to 8 minutes. Add the rest of the vegetables, and sauté for 10 more minutes.

Add the stock and salt to the sautéed vegetables. Bring the stock to a boil and then reduce it to a simmer. Simmer the soup for 30 minutes. Cool the soup slightly and then puree it in a blender, working in small batches to avoid an explosion of hot liquid.

Return the soup to the pot and add the half-and-half and herbs. Taste, adjust the seasoning as needed, and either serve the soup immediately or simmer it gently until serving time, being careful not to let the soup boil.

Kale and Potato Soup

Kale and potato soup is a traditional soup of Portugal. With the addition of white beans, it is called caldo verde. The beans add protein and a rich, creamy texture. If you use beans, you will need more stock or water. **// SERVES 6 TO 8**

3 tablespoons olive oil
1 large onion, chopped
4 cloves garlic, chopped
Pinch of red pepper flakes
3 medium potatoes, cubed
4 cups water or vegetable stock
1 teaspoon salt
1 bunch kale, washed, stemmed, and torn into pieces
3 tablespoons soy sauce
Freshly ground pepper
1 (15-ounce) can white beans, drained and rinsed (optional)

Heat the oil in a soup pot. Sauté the onions until they are soft. Add the garlic and red pepper flakes and sauté for another minute. Add the potatoes along with the stock and salt.

Bring the stock to a boil; then lower the heat and simmer until the potatoes are soft, about 8 to 10 minutes.

Add the kale, soy sauce, and pepper. Simmer for 4 to 5 minutes. Add the white beans (if using). Add a little more stock or water as needed for the desired consistency.

New (freshly dug) potatoes taste of summer. Once cured, they are a staple of the winter pantry.

Roasted Potato–Garlic Soup

*Roasting vegetables really brings out their flavors. Once roasted, what seems like a lot of garlic really has a delicate flavor. You can add cream or soy milk if you like, but the soup is great without it. We like to serve this soup with pumpernickel bread and a sharp cheddar cheese. // * **SERVES 6 TO 8**

6 medium red potatoes
1 large onion
2 tablespoons olive oil
3 heads garlic
5 cups vegetable stock or water
1 cup half-and-half or soy milk (optional)
1½ teaspoons salt
Freshly ground pepper

Preheat the oven to 400 degrees.

Peel the potatoes, leaving on about a third of the peel. Cut the potatoes into 1-inch pieces; you should have 6 cups. Roughly chop the onion. Mix the potato and onion in a large bowl with the olive oil, stirring until well coated. Spread the vegetables on a sheet pan and bake for approximately 40 minutes, or until thoroughly done.

You can roast the garlic at the same time as the potatoes and onion. Put the whole heads of garlic directly on the oven shelf or on the sheet pan if there is room. Roast them for about 30 minutes, or until they are very soft. Let the garlic cool a bit; then hold the bottom of the bulb and squeeze the cooked garlic into a bowl.

Hardneck garlic, much of it native to states of the former USSR, thrives in the Upper Midwest.

Working in small batches, combine the potatoes, onions, garlic, stock, and half-and-half (if using) in a blender. Blend until the soup is slightly chunky, but not creamy (be careful not to overpuree). If the soup is thicker than you would like, add a little more stock or half-and-half to thin it.

Pour the soup into a large saucepan. Add salt and pepper to taste and heat until the soup is warmed through, being careful not to let the soup boil.

Squash and Wild Rice Soup

We love squash in soup. It's not difficult to use. Make this comforting fall soup when your local farmers' market is loaded with winter squash. Kabocha, butternut, and buttercup are wonderful varieties to try. See the note about wild rice in the grains section (page 86) for clarification on the different types of and cooking times for wild rice. // SERVES 6

1 tablespoon vegetable oil or olive oil
1 large onion, chopped (2 cups)
1 cup diced celery
1 winter squash, peeled and cut into 1-inch pieces (3 cups)
¾ cup parched wild rice

2 tablespoons fresh sage or 1½ teaspoons dried
1½ teaspoons salt
8 cups vegetable stock or water
1 tablespoon soy sauce

Rinse the wild rice well. If you are using paddy rice instead of parched wild rice, simmer it for about 25 minutes so it is partially cooked before you add it to the soup pot. Parched wild rice doesn't need to be precooked.

Heat the oil in a soup pot. Add the onions and sauté until they are soft. Add the celery, squash, wild rice, sage, salt, stock, and soy sauce. Bring the stock to a boil; then turn down the heat and simmer for 25 minutes, until the rice is tender.

Quinoa Corn Soup

This soup can be made with fresh or frozen sweet corn. When sweet corn is in season, use two large ears, cutting the kernels off the cob for the soup and reserving the cobs to make stock (page 24).
// SERVES 6 TO 8

8 cups water or vegetable stock
½ cup quinoa, rinsed well
1 (10-ounce) bag frozen sweet corn or 2 ears fresh
    sweet corn
1 medium onion, finely diced
2 carrots, sliced

2 stalks celery, diced
1½ teaspoons salt
1 teaspoon chopped fresh parsley
1 teaspoon chopped fresh oregano or marjoram or
    ½ teaspoon dried
Cilantro or ancho chili powder, for garnish

Combine the water, quinoa, and frozen corn in a soup pot and bring it to a boil. Reduce the heat and simmer for 5 minutes.

Add the onions, carrots, celery, salt, parsley, and oregano and continue cooking for another 8 to 10 minutes. Garnish with fresh chopped cilantro or, for a smoky hot touch, add a pinch of ancho chili powder.

Quinoa Corn Soup

Golden Grain Soup

This is a hearty, earthy soup. It is filling and easily becomes a full meal when served with bread and cheese or a nice green salad. The soup needs to simmer a long time to fully cook the grains. This makes it very easy to digest as well as very flavorful. You can cook it early in the day and reheat it when you are ready to serve. // **SERVES 6 TO 8**

¼ cup brown rice
¼ cup pearled barley
2 tablespoons vegetable oil or olive oil
2 medium onions, chopped (2 cups)
½ cup chopped celery
8 ounces mushrooms, sliced

8 cups vegetable stock
½ cup soy sauce
2 bay leaves
⅓ cup rolled oats
Freshly ground pepper
2 to 3 tablespoons chopped parsley

Rinse the rice and the barley and set them aside.

Heat the oil in a soup pot and sauté the onions until they are soft. Add the celery and sauté another 3 to 5 minutes; then add the sliced mushrooms and sauté them for a few minutes. Add the stock, rice, barley, soy sauce, bay leaves, and oats.

Bring the stock to a boil and then turn down the heat to a low simmer. Cook for one hour. Taste to determine whether the grains have fully cooked. Simmer a little longer if necessary. Add pepper and parsley to taste.

Tim's Miso Soup

Brenda's husband, Tim, makes miso soup for breakfast, which is very common in Japan. Savory and strengthening, miso soup is a great way to start the day and a healthy alternative to a latte and a cinnamon roll. // **SERVES 4 TO 6**

⅓ cup brown miso
¼ cup white miso
7 cups water
1 teaspoon wakame flakes
1 cup peeled, seeded, and diced squash or carrots
1 cup sliced leeks, washed well

1 cup sliced cabbage
1 daikon radish, peeled, cut lengthwise, and sliced into
    half-moons (½ cup)
½ bunch kale, stemmed and cut into 1-inch pieces
    (2 cups)

Place the miso in 1 cup of the water and stir to dissolve it. Set it aside for now. (You may use just one kind of miso. The brown miso has a stronger taste than the white.)

Combine the remaining water, wakame, and squash in a soup pot. Bring the water to a boil. Add the leeks and cabbage, and reduce the heat to a simmer. Simmer for 1 minute, and then add the daikon. After another minute, add the kale. Cook for 1 to 2 more minutes. Add the dissolved miso and cook gently for a few more minutes.

Split Pea–Kale Soup

We like this one-pot pea soup. Adding kale is a good way to bring even more nutrients into this classic split pea soup. // **SERVES 8**

1 pound (2 cups) split peas
9 cups water or vegetable stock
1 onion, diced
2 carrots, sliced or diced (1 cup)
2 stalks celery, diced

1 teaspoon dried thyme or parsley
½ bunch kale, stemmed and cut into 1-inch pieces
    (2 cups)
1 tablespoon salt

Sort through the split peas, picking out any small stones or dirt. Wash the peas and put them into a soup pot. Add the water and bring it to a boil. Skim off and discard any foam that rises to the top.

Add the onions, carrots, celery, and herbs. Simmer over medium-low heat for approximately 50 minutes or until the peas are soft. Add the kale and salt during the last 3 minutes.

Lentil Barley Vegetable Soup

This quintessential paring of a grain and a legume results in a complete protein. Adding kale, collards, or mustard greens, which appear on many superfood lists, makes this soup a meal in itself. // **SERVES 8**

1 cup lentils
¼ cup barley
8 cups water
1 tablespoon olive oil
1 large onion, diced
4 cloves garlic, minced
2 large carrots, diced

2 stalks celery, diced
1 (14-ounce) can of crushed tomatoes
2 tablespoons soy sauce
1 teaspoon salt
1 large bunch kale, collards, or mustard greens, stemmed
    and chopped (4 cups)
2 tablespoons chopped fresh parsley or basil

Clean the lentils and barley and put them in a large soup pot with the water. Bring the water to a boil, and then reduce the heat to a simmer and cook, covered, for 40 minutes.

In another pan, heat the olive oil and sauté the onions and garlic for a few minutes. Add the carrots and celery, and sauté a few minutes longer.

Add the sautéed vegetables, tomatoes, soy sauce, and salt to the lentils and barley and simmer for 15 minutes.

Add the kale and herbs, and cook for 5 more minutes.

Black-Eyed Pea Soup with Greens

Black-eyed peas have a mild flavor and go well with greens. They do not need to be soaked, but black-eyed peas will cook faster if you do soak them. This soup is full of vegetables, making it flavorful and filling. Black-eyed peas are the principal component of hoppin' John, which is served in the South on New Year's Day to bring luck for the new year. We like to think that this soup nourishes us, bringing us luck throughout the year. // SERVES 4 TO 6

2 tablespoons olive oil or vegetable oil
1 medium onion, chopped
4 cloves garlic, chopped
1 cup dried black-eyed peas
1 teaspoon dried thyme
1 teaspoon ground cumin
½ teaspoon red pepper flakes or 1 teaspoon smoked paprika
10 cups vegetable stock or water
1 red bell pepper, diced
1 stalk celery, chopped
1 large carrot, chopped
1 teaspoon salt
½ bunch kale or chard or 1 bunch spinach, stemmed and chopped (2 cups slightly packed)

Black-Eyed Pea Soup with Greens

Heat 1 tablespoon of the vegetable oil in a soup pot. When it is hot, add the onions and garlic, and sauté over medium heat for 4 to 5 minutes.

Add the black-eyed peas, thyme, cumin, red pepper flakes, and stock and bring it to a boil. Cover and simmer for 30 minutes.

In a separate pan, heat the remaining 1 tablespoon of oil and sauté the red bell pepper, celery, and carrots for 6 to 8 minutes, stirring occasionally.

Add the sautéed vegetables and salt to the soup pot. Simmer for 15 minutes. Add the greens to the pot just before serving, allowing 4 to 5 minutes for kale to cook or 2 minutes for chard or spinach to cook.

Lemon–Lima Bean Soup

If you think you don't like lima beans, this soup will win you over. It's a simple and straightforward variation of traditional Greek avgolemono. // **SERVES 6 TO 8**

5 cups cooked lima beans (2 cups dried)
2 tablespoons butter or olive oil
1 large onion, coarsely chopped
2 stalks celery, diced
8 cups vegetable stock

2 teaspoons salt
1½ teaspoons dried sage
Zest of 1 lemon
¼ cup fresh lemon juice

If you are using dried lima beans, soak the beans for 3 to 4 hours. Rinse the beans and place them in a large saucepan with enough water to cover the beans completely. Bring to a boil; then reduce the heat and simmer for 30 minutes. Drain the beans. The beans will not be quite done but will continue to cook in the soup. Remove any skins that have slipped off the beans.

Melt the butter in a large sauté pan. Cook the onions slowly for 30 minutes over medium to low heat, stirring often, until they are caramelized. If the onions start to stick to the pan, turn down the heat.

Add the celery and continue sautéing for another 5 minutes, until the celery is soft.

Combine the beans, stock, and sautéed vegetables in a large soup pot. Add the salt, sage, and lemon zest. Bring the soup to a boil and then reduce the heat. Gently simmer for 20 to 30 minutes. Add the lemon juice just before serving.

Minestrone

There are as many versions of minestrone as there are regions of Italy; however, they all contain lots of vegetables and some kind of bean. We also like this version made with lentils. This is very good the second day, as all bean soups are, but it will thicken up as it sits. // **SERVES 4 TO 6**

1 tablespoon olive oil
1 small onion, chopped
1 stalk celery, diced
1 carrot, diced
1 large potato, peeled and cubed (1 cup)
2 medium tomatoes, diced, or 1 (14.5-ounce) can
    diced tomatoes
2 teaspoons cumin seeds

8 cups vegetable stock
5 ounces dried pasta (1 cup)
1 small zucchini, diced
1½ cups cooked white beans or 1 (15-ounce) can white
    beans, drained and rinsed
1 teaspoon salt
½ teaspoon pepper
1 teaspoon dried basil or 2 tablespoons chopped fresh basil

Heat the olive oil in a soup pot. Sauté the onion until it is soft. Add the celery and carrots, and continue cooking another 5 minutes. Add the potatoes, tomatoes, cumin, and stock. Bring to a low boil, and then turn down the heat and simmer for 15 minutes.

While the soup is simmering, cook the pasta in a separate saucepan until just al dente. The pasta will cook some more in the soup. You can cook the pasta directly in the soup, but by cooking it separately you have more control over how well cooked it is and the soup will not be as starchy.

Add the zucchini, beans, salt, and pepper to the soup pot, and cook for another 10 minutes. Add the precooked pasta and let the soup simmer for another 5 minutes. (If you are not serving the soup right away or plan to have leftovers, add pasta only to the soup you are serving. Store the cooked pasta separately and add it when reheating the soup.) Add the basil and taste the soup, adjusting the seasoning if needed.

Top with grated Parmesan cheese, if you like.

Minestrone

Black Bean Soup

This is an earthy soup with a rich bean flavor. It is a meal in itself when served with tortillas or cornbread and a salad. If you are using canned beans, this is a super quick and easy preparation. Whenever we cook black beans, we add soy sauce; they complement each other beautifully.

Cooking beans in a pressure cooker is so much quicker than cooking them in a soup pot, and they turn out so plump and velvety. You can cut the cooking time to 25 minutes for unsoaked beans. We highly recommend buying a pressure cooker if you are incorporating a good amount of wonderful beans into your diet and you're not cooking for one. They are not dangerous and can often be found at rummage sales and garage sales because people are intimidated by them. Purchase only stainless steel though. **// SERVES 6 TO 8**

1 cup dried beans (3 cups cooked) or 2 (15-ounce) cans black beans, drained and rinsed

1 tablespoon olive oil or vegetable oil

1 onion, diced

4 cloves garlic, chopped

1 stalk celery, diced

2 large carrots, diced

1 teaspoon cumin

1 teaspoon oregano

¼ teaspoon cayenne

1 teaspoon salt

4–5 cups vegetable stock or water

1 (15-ounce) can of tomatoes or 1½ cups diced fresh tomatoes, if in season

2 tablespoons tomato paste

1 tablespoon soy sauce

Sour cream and cilantro, for garnish

If you are using dried beans, sort through the beans to remove any rocks or debris. Soak the beans for at least 4 hours in enough water to cover them. Rinse and drain the beans, put them in a pot with water to cover, and cook until they are tender, about 1 hour.

Heat the oil and sauté the onions and garlic until the onions are soft. Add the celery, carrots, cumin, oregano, cayenne, and salt. Sauté until the carrots are tender, about 5 minutes.

Combine the beans, stock, and sautéed vegetables in a large soup pot. Add the tomatoes, tomato paste, and soy sauce. Adjust the seasonings to taste. Simmer for 15 minutes.

Garnish with sour cream and cilantro.

Pinto Bean–Lime Soup

The flavor combination of lime, beans, and cilantro will transport you to Mexico without the expensive ticket. Cornbread is a perfect accompaniment.

We like to add some fresh herbs and celery when cooking the beans. You may substitute other herbs; use what you have on hand. Keep the herbs and celery in large pieces so they are easy to remove after cooking the beans. // **SERVES 6 TO 8**

1¼ cups dried pinto beans, soaked 6 hours or overnight, or 2 (15-ounce) cans pinto beans, drained
1 bay leaf
Several sprigs of fresh thyme and parsley, or 1 teaspoon each dried
3 stalks celery, 1 cut in half and 2 diced
1 tablespoon vegetable oil or olive oil

1 small onion, chopped
4 cups vegetable stock or water with a splash of soy sauce
1 teaspoon salt
1 teaspoon ground cumin
2 tablespoons lime juice
Freshly ground pepper
5 green onions or a small bunch of chives, chopped

If you are using dried beans, rinse and drain the beans. Place them in a saucepan with 5 cups of water and the bay leaf, thyme and parsley sprigs, and halved stalk of celery. Bring the water to a boil; then turn down the heat and simmer over medium-low heat for 1½ hours, until beans are just tender but not soft and falling apart. The beans will cook some more in the soup. Drain the beans and remove the herbs and celery.

Heat the vegetable oil in a soup pot and sauté the onions until soft. Add the diced celery and sauté until the celery is tender, about 3 to 5 minutes. Add the vegetable stock, salt, cumin, and lime juice. Bring to a boil; then turn down the heat to medium-low. Add the beans and simmer for 30 minutes. Add the pepper and green onions just before serving.

Garnish with sour cream, cilantro, and lime slices.

Red Bean Mushroom Soup

This soup takes a turn from the traditional bean soup. The woodsy mushroom and ginger flavors are perfect complements to the red beans. If you happen to have fresh or dried shitakes, use them instead of or in addition to the button mushrooms. They will add richness to the soup. // **SERVES 6 TO 8**

1 medium onion, diced
2 tablespoons vegetable oil or olive oil
2 large carrots, peeled and diced
1 stalk celery, diced
8 ounces mushrooms, sliced
5 to 6 cloves garlic, crushed

2 tablespoons finely chopped ginger
5 cups vegetable stock or water
1 (15-ounce) can red beans
¼ cup soy sauce
Salt
¼ teaspoon cayenne

Sauté the onion in the vegetable oil. When the onions are soft, add the carrots and celery and sauté for 3 minutes more. Add the mushrooms, garlic, and ginger and sauté another 3 to 5 minutes.

Combine the stock, beans, and sautéed vegetables in a large soup pot. Add the soy sauce, salt, and cayenne. Bring the soup to a simmer and cook until soup is heated through and the flavors combine.

Tomato White Bean Soup

White miso adds a trace of sweetness without added sugar. The hint of cardamom points this soup east, slightly away from its traditional Italian roots. **// SERVES 6 TO 8**

2 tablespoons olive oil
1 large onion, diced
4 cloves garlic, sliced
8 cups water or vegetable stock
2 carrots, sliced
1 (28-ounce) can diced tomatoes

1 (15-ounce) can cannellini beans, rinsed
1 tablespoon white miso (optional)
3 tablespoons chopped parsley
¼ teaspoon ground cardamom
Salt
Pepper

Heat the olive oil in a soup pot. Add the onions and garlic and sauté for a few minutes. Add the water, carrots, and tomatoes. Bring to a simmer and cook for approximately 20 minutes, until the vegetables are soft.

Add the beans. Working in small batches to avoid an explosion of hot liquid, puree the soup in a blender until it is smooth and return it to the soup pot.

Add the miso (if using), parsley, and cardamom and heat the soup to a simmer. Season with salt and pepper before serving.

Chickpea Pumpkin Soup

Pumpkin soup is a fall favorite of ours. This recipe uses chickpeas and oatmeal for a hearty, rich flavor. When small baking pumpkins are not available, use winter squash. Choose one full of flavor such as buttercup squash. // SERVES 6

1 small pumpkin or winter squash (5 to 6 cups cubed)
2 tablespoons olive oil or vegetable oil
1 medium onion, coarsely chopped
5 cups vegetable stock or water
1½ teaspoons salt
½ teaspoon dried thyme
¼ cup rolled oats
1 (15-ounce) can chickpeas or 1½ cups cooked

Peel the pumpkin (use the peelings for making stock) and cut it in half. Clean out the seeds and stringy portion, and cut the flesh into 1-inch pieces. You should have 5 to 6 cups of pumpkin.

Heat the oil in a soup pot and sauté the onions until soft. Add the pumpkin and sauté for an additional 10 minutes.

Add the stock, salt, thyme, and rolled oats. Cover the pot and simmer over medium heat until the pumpkin is tender, approximately 30 minutes. Add the chickpeas and continue cooking for another 10 to 15 minutes. If you prefer a soup with some texture, serve it while the pumpkin still has some shape to it. If you want a creamy soup, let the soup continue to cook until the pumpkin falls apart into a puree.

White Bean and Squash Soup

This soup manages to be delicate in flavor yet very hearty. When pureed, winter squash lends a buttery richness without adding any dairy. // **SERVES 6**

1 tablespoon olive oil or butter
4 cloves garlic, chopped
1 medium onion, chopped
1 winter squash, peeled, seeded, and cut into 1-inch cubes
  (3½ cups), or 1 (10-ounce) package frozen squash
1 (15-ounce) can navy beans or 1½ cups cooked beans

½ teaspoon dried basil or oregano
¼ teaspoon dried thyme
4 cups vegetable stock or water
¼ teaspoon salt
Pepper

Heat the oil in a soup pot and sauté the garlic and onions for approximately 5 minutes.

Add the cubed squash, cooked beans, basil, thyme, stock, and salt. Bring the stock to a boil; then reduce the heat and simmer until the squash is tender, approximately 20 minutes.

Working in small batches, puree the soup in a blender or put it through a food mill. Return it to the soup pot. Taste the soup and adjust the seasoning, adding more salt if needed and pepper to taste. Bring the soup back to a simmer and serve.

Matzo Ball Soup

Some like their matzo balls firm, others prefer them light. Play around with the recipe if you prefer a firmer texture. We just love soup with lots of vegetables; please make sure you add them all. We could eat this soup every week. This soup is just as delicious made with vegetable stock as with chicken stock. **// SERVES 6 LARGE PORTIONS**

MATZO BALLS //

1 tablespoon olive oil
3 tablespoons water
2 medium eggs, slightly beaten
1 teaspoon salt
½ cup matzo meal

SOUP //

1 tablespoon olive oil
4 to 6 cloves garlic, minced
2 medium-size onions, thickly sliced
2 cups peeled and thickly sliced rutabagas
1½ cups thickly sliced carrots
2 stalks celery, sliced
8 cups chicken stock or vegetable stock
1 teaspoon salt
½ bunch kale, stemmed and cut into 1-inch pieces (2 cups)
Pepper

To make the matzo balls, whisk together the oil, water, eggs, and salt in a bowl, and then stir in matzo meal. Refrigerate the dough for 15 minutes.

Form the dough into balls that are about 1 inch in diameter.

To make the soup, heat the oil in a soup pot. Sauté the garlic, onions, and rutabagas for 3 minutes. Add the carrots and celery and sauté for 3 more minutes. Add the stock and bring it to a boil. Add the salt.

Now drop in the matzo balls. Turn down the heat and simmer, covered, for 30 minutes. Add the kale and season with pepper to taste. Cover the pot and let the kale steam for 3 to 4 minutes, until tender.

Turkey Wild Rice Soup

Turkey and wild rice combine to make a hearty, flavorful soup. You can use leftover cooked turkey meat or buy a turkey breast or some thighs to make this soup. This soup could also be made with chicken. // **SERVES 6**

⅔ cup wild rice
1 cup diced yellow onion
2 tablespoons olive oil
2 carrots, diced (1 cup)
1½ stalks celery, diced (¾ cup)
½ tablespoon minced garlic
½ teaspoon turmeric

1 teaspoon dried thyme
½ teaspoon salt
Pepper
8 cups chicken stock or vegetable stock
2 cups diced raw turkey
¼ cup chopped fresh parsley

Cook the wild rice following the directions on the package. The cooking time will vary depending on the type of rice. Roasted, or parched, wild rice will take about 20 minutes, while the darker, shiny unroasted rice will take up to 50 minutes.

Sauté the onions in the olive oil for 3 to 4 minutes. Add the carrots, celery, garlic, turmeric, thyme, salt, and pepper. Continue cooking for another 5 minutes. Add the stock and turkey. (If you are using cooked turkey, add it later, with the rice.)

Simmer over medium heat until the vegetables and turkey are cooked, about 15 minutes. Add the cooked rice and parsley. Simmer for a few more minutes.

Red Lentil Vegetable Soup

Red lentils are a terrific ingredient because they are quick cooking and have a wonderful texture and color. This vegetable-packed soup is a very simple-to-prepare crowd pleaser. **// SERVES 8**

1½ tablespoons olive oil or vegetable oil
1 onion, diced fine
½ teaspoon fennel seeds
1½ cups red lentils, sorted and rinsed
¾ cup chopped canned or fresh tomatoes
7 cups water
2 carrots, sliced
1 cup cauliflower pieces
1 stalk celery, diced
2 teaspoons salt
¼ cup chopped parsley (optional)

Heat the oil in a soup pot. Add the onions and fennel seeds and sauté for 5 to 7 minutes over medium heat. Add the lentils, tomatoes, and water and bring to a boil. Turn down the heat and simmer for 25 to 30 minutes. Add the carrots, cauliflower, celery, and salt. Simmer for another 10 minutes, or until the vegetables are soft and the lentils have fallen apart. Add the chopped parsley (if using) after the soup is done cooking.

Cauliflower and romanesco

salads

Basil Honey Dressing

This incredibly bright dressing, not your typical vinaigrette, is a wonderful summer treat. Garnish your salad with strawberries and toasted nuts. Feel free to substitute rice vinegar or champagne vinegar if you do not have white balsamic vinegar on hand. // **MAKES ABOUT 3 CUPS**

1 cup packed basil leaves
¼ cup coarsely chopped onion
1 tablespoon dry mustard

3 tablespoons honey
1 cup white balsamic vinegar or lemon juice
1 cup olive oil

Place all of the ingredients in a blender and blend until smooth.

Pomegranate Dressing

Pomegranate's health benefits are much touted these days. This fragrant, flowery, Middle Eastern dressing is almost like aromatherapy. It goes exceedingly well with spinach. **// MAKES 1½ CUPS**

1 tablespoon pomegranate molasses
⅓ cup apple juice or another juice other than orange
¼ cup red or white wine vinegar
1 tablespoon honey

1 tablespoon chopped mint or basil
1 teaspoon rose water
½ teaspoon salt
¾ cup mild olive oil or vegetable oil

Whisk together the pomegranate molasses, apple juice, vinegar, honey, mint, rose water, and salt. Pour in the oil in a slow, steady stream while whisking constantly.

POMEGRANATE MOLASSES //

Pomegranate molasses is really delicious in salad dressings and in marinades for lamb, chicken, and fish (see Broiled Fresh Rainbow Trout with Pomegranate Brown Butter Sauce, page 162). It can be drizzled on dishes as you would a nice balsamic vinegar reduction. It has a tangy, sour side to it, though. Pomegranate molasses has a bright taste that can be a great accent to desserts as well; just a thin swirl on the plate will do you! If you don't have a bottle of pomegranate molasses, you will want to go on a field trip to to an import store or Middle Eastern market to find some. The rose water will be right next to it on the shelf—grab one of those too. And if you see orange blossom water nearby, don't pass a bottle of that up either. They will last on your shelf a year or longer. Trust me.

Oil-Free Dressing

Not all salad dressings need to be based on a ratio of oil to acid. Lighter oil-free dressings provide sweetness and tang with juices, sweet wines, and vinegars. They also can give some salads a pickled quality, as with thinly sliced cucumbers. Try fruit juices reduced to a third or a quarter of their volume. The thicker juice is not only sweeter but coats the vegetables better. // **MAKES ABOUT 1 CUP**

SALADS

1 cup of apple juice
¼ cup mirin
¼ cup rice vinegar

Juice of ½ orange
¼ teaspoon salt
Pepper

Pour the apple juice into a saucepan and bring it to a boil. Simmer until the juice has reduced to about ⅓ cup.

Combine the reduced apple juice in a bowl with the mirin, rice vinegar, orange juice, and salt and mix together with a whisk. Add pepper to taste.

Sesame Vinaigrette

A very nutty, toasted sesame flavor combined with a hint of honey, vinegar, and ginger adds a wonderful flair to any Asian-influenced salad or meal. **II MAKES 1 CUP**

½ cup rice vinegar
1½ tablespoons honey
1 tablespoon toasted sesame oil
2 teaspoons soy sauce

1 tablespoon finely grated ginger
Pinch of cayenne (optional)
½ cup plus 1 tablespoon vegetable oil

Combine the vinegar, honey, sesame oil, soy sauce, ginger, and cayenne (if using) in a small bowl and whisk to combine. Slowly pour in the oil while whisking. Continue whisking until the oil is well incorporated.

White Balsamic Vinaigrette

White balsamic vinegar is lower in acid than most other vinegars, which allows you to use less oil in a dressing. We have found beautiful white balsamic vinegars, even one that tastes like fresh strawberries! We really like how fresh and light this dressing is. // **MAKES 2 CUPS**

¾ cup white balsamic vinegar
1 heaping tablespoon chopped fresh tarragon
½ tablespoon Dijon mustard
1 medium clove garlic, minced
½ tablespoon honey

¼ teaspoon pepper
1 teaspoon salt
Zest and juice of half a lemon (optional)
1 cup olive oil

Mix together the vinegar, tarragon, mustard, garlic, honey, pepper, salt, and lemon zest and juice (if using). Add the oil in a steady stream while whisking.

Citrus Vinaigrette

This is an all-purpose vinaigrette for salad greens and blanched vegetables. Try it on fresh blanched green beans with lemon zest. You can use all vegetable oil or use part nut oil or olive oil. Try making it with walnut or pumpkin seed oil, and toss toasted walnuts or pumpkin seeds on your salad.

// MAKES ⅔ CUP

2 tablespoons lemon juice
¼ cup grapefruit or orange juice
4 tablespoons vegetable oil or 2 tablespoons vegetable oil
    plus 2 tablespoons nut or olive oil

1 small shallot, minced
Salt and pepper

Combine all of the ingredients in a bowl and whisk until well mixed. Store the dressing in the refrigerator.

SALADS AND HOMEMADE DRESSING //

Buy whole heads of Bibb, leaf, and romaine lettuce and wash them. This will usually save you money, and you will end up with a much fresher salad than with the prewashed bagged salad mixes (which you really should wash anyway). Some of our favorite simple additions to greens include:

grated carrots (no need to peel them)
thinly sliced red cabbage
thinly sliced fennel crisped in cold water for a while
red or sweet white onions
green onions
radishes
thinly sliced cucumbers
avocado
alfalfa, clover, broccoli, or other sprouts
arugula
berries
orange or grapefruit pieces
apples or pears
nuts, such as walnuts, pistachios, toasted almonds,
    and pumpkin seeds
chickpeas (canned are fine)
goat cheese, feta, or bleu cheese

Dressings

A simple vinegar and oil dressing uses about 1 part vinegar to 3 parts oil. We sometimes like to use fresh citrus, apple, or any number of juices instead of all vinegar. Replacing some of the vinegar with juice allows for a lighter dressing because you can add less oil. Try adding mirin, honey, or a splash of maple syrup for a touch of sweetness. Mustard adds a spark of spiciness, but dissolve it in the other ingredients before adding the oil.

Arugula

Caesar Salad Dressing

A delicious Caesar salad needs high-quality Parmesan and good olive oil. When possible, buy a whole head of fresh green romaine and take care to wash and crisp it in advance of serving.
// MAKES 1¼ CUPS

2 medium-small anchovies, rinsed well and minced
2 cloves garlic, chopped
1 egg
Freshly ground pepper
⅓ cup grated Parmesan
3 tablespoons fresh lemon juice
Pinch of cayenne
¼ teaspoon salt
⅓ cup olive oil
⅓ cup sunflower or vegetable oil

Romaine

Combine the anchovies, garlic, egg, and pepper in a food processor or blender. Process until well mixed. Add the Parmesan. Mix again. Add the lemon juice, cayenne, and salt and process briefly.

Slowly add the oil while the machine is running. This allows an emulsion to form. Add more oil if the mixture is too runny. The dressing keeps one week in the refrigerator.

Greek Black-Eyed Pea Salad

This is a nice summer salad. If you do not have pomegranate molasses, you can omit it, but it is a nice thing to have in your pantry. It lasts a long time and is a great addition to marinades, dressings, and vinaigrettes. It adds a rich tangy flavor. You can find it in import stores or Middle Eastern markets. // **SERVES 6**

SALAD //

1½ cups black-eyed peas
½ bunch green onions, sliced
½ pint cherry tomatoes, halved
1 bunch parsley, chopped
½ cup lightly packed mint leaves, chopped
½ cup green or black olives
Lettuce, for serving

Wash the black-eyed peas, put them in a pot, and add enough water to cover them. Bring the water to a boil; then turn down the heat and simmer until the black-eyed peas are tender, approximately 30 minutes.

In a large bowl, combine the black-eyed peas with the green onions, tomatoes, parsley, mint, and olives.

DRESSING //

3 tablespoons red wine vinegar
2 tablespoons lemon juice
½ tablespoon Dijon mustard
½ tablespoon pomegranate molasses or balsamic vinegar
⅓ cup extra-virgin olive oil
½ tablespoon minced garlic
1½ teaspoons salt
Freshly ground pepper

To make the dressing, whisk together the vinegar, lemon juice, and mustard. Then add the pomegranate molasses, olive oil, garlic, salt, and pepper. Whisk until well mixed.

Toss the dressing with the salad. Let the salad marinate at least 30 minutes before serving it on a bed of lettuce.

Tiny, but full of flavor

Lentil and Mint Salad

Lentils are a terrific source of protein. Their rich taste and quick cooking time make them a great choice for a meal designed around a legume. We prefer a simple brown lentil for this. French lentils are also very good but can take a little longer to cook; red lentils don't work for this recipe. Add a half cup of feta or fresh goat cheese and some olives if you like. Serve the salad on a bed of lettuce with bread for a great meal. // **SERVES 4 TO 6**

1 cup lentils
3 tablespoons olive oil
½ cup diced onion
1 stalk celery, diced (⅓ cup)
1 carrot, diced (½ cup)
1 tablespoon red wine vinegar

½ teaspoon salt
Freshly ground pepper
2 tablespoons chopped parsley
2 tablespoons chopped fresh mint
Feta or chèvre cheese (optional)
Olives (optional)

Sort through the lentils to make sure there are no little stones in them. Rinse the lentils well and then place them in a saucepan with 4 cups water. Bring the water to a boil; then turn down the heat and simmer until the lentils are tender, about 35 minutes, longer if needed.

Heat 1 tablespoon of the oil in a sauté pan. Sauté the onions for 3 to 4 minutes. Add the celery and carrots and continue cooking until they are tender, about 5 minutes.

When the lentils are done, toss them with the vinegar, salt, and pepper. Add the remaining 2 tablespoons of olive oil and stir well. Stir in the sautéed vegetables, parsley, mint, and feta and olives (if using). Taste the salad and add more salt or pepper as needed.

SANDRA JEAN'S HERB FARM //

Sandra Jean's Herb Farm has been growing for me since my daughter, Celina, was one year old (she's in college now). We meet every spring to decide what worked best next season, what we want her to grow for us this year, and in what quantity. When I see Sandra Jean, I know that we are nearly finished with the long winter. She is better than any robin at providing a sure sign that spring is arriving.

Sandra Jean grows arugula, amazing varieties of kale, Swiss chard, spinach, green beans, peas, eggplant, tomatoes, raspberries, and all of our fresh herbs. She also keeps chickens and supplies us with eggs in a wonderful array of colors.

Sandra and her son Elijah love their new tractor.

Brenda admires one of the wonderful varieties of kale on Sandra Jean's farm near South Haven, Minnesota.

SALADS

Orzo Pistachio Salad

Figs and pistachios combine with pasta to create a refreshing, light pasta salad. You could also make this with almonds and golden raisins. // **SERVES 4 TO 6**

½ cup dried black figs
½ teaspoon turmeric
½ pound (1¼ cups) orzo
½ cup pistachios, coarsely chopped
⅓ cup fresh mint, chopped
3 green onions, sliced thin

2 tablespoons lemon juice
Zest of half a lemon
2 tablespoons olive oil
¾ teaspoon salt
Pepper

Place the figs in a small bowl and cover them with boiling water. Let them sit in the water for 30 minutes, until the figs are plump. Drain the figs well and then chop them. You can skip the soaking if you have plump, moist figs.

Put some water and the turmeric in a large saucepan and bring to a boil. Add the orzo and cook it for 7 to 9 minutes, or until tender. Drain the orzo and set it aside. Do not rinse it.

Toss the orzo with the figs, pistachios, mint, and green onions.

In a small bowl, combine the lemon juice, zest, olive oil, and salt. Stir this dressing into the orzo salad. Add pepper to taste.

White Bean Tuna Salad

This is a French-inspired summer salad. It is delicious served as a first course, or garnish it with hard-boiled eggs, olives, and cherry tomatoes and serve it with a good crusty bread for a complete meal. Buy the best quality tuna you can get; you'll be surprised at how good canned tuna can be. // **SERVES 4**

1 (6-ounce) can water-packed tuna, drained
1 (15-ounce) can white beans, drained and rinsed
⅓ cup diced red onion
1 stalk celery, diced (⅓ cup)
2 tablespoons chopped fresh parsley
1 tablespoon olive oil
1½ tablespoons red wine vinegar

1 large clove garlic, minced
½ teaspoon salt
Freshly ground pepper
½ teaspoon fennel seeds
Fresh greens, for serving
Hard-boiled eggs, olives, and cherry tomatoes, for garnish

Combine the tuna and beans in a bowl. Add the red onion, celery, and parsley. Stir gently. Add the oil, vinegar, garlic, salt, and pepper.

Toast the fennel seeds in a dry pan for a few minutes until they are fragrant. Do not let the seeds brown. Coarsely chop the seeds. Add them to the salad and stir well to incorporate the oil and vinegar.

Serve the salad on fresh greens, and garnish it with hard-boiled eggs, olives, and cherry tomatoes.

Shaved Vegetable Salad

This very colorful salad with thinly shaved vegetable ribbons is an elegant accompaniment to any meal. Take special care to crisp your vegetables for at least an hour before assembling and serving the salad.

// SERVES 4 TO 6

2 medium carrots (in rainbow colors, if you can find them)
2 to 3 wide stalks celery
3 to 4 radishes, leave a little stem on

1 cucumber
White Balsamic Vinaigrette (page 66)
2 cups microgreens

Peel the carrots. Then, starting at the top and going all the way down to the bottom, use the peeler to cut thin sheets of carrot. Do not turn the carrot at all.

Peel off the outer, stringy part of the celery and discard it. Again, use the peeler to cut long, straight strips of celery.

Slice the radishes as thinly as possible.

Peel the cucumber; then cut long strips, turning the cucumber to get nice wide pieces while avoiding the seeds. Throw the seeds away.

Put the vegetable slices in a bowl of cold water for at least an hour to crisp and curl.

Gently toss the vegetables with a light coating of White Balsamic Vinaigrette just before serving. Serve the vegetables on a bed of microgreens.

Shaved Vegetable Salad

Wild Rice, Vegetable, and Smoked Trout Salad

The earthy Northwoods flavors of wild rice and smoked trout are wonderful together. The best time to serve this salad is when you can garnish it with fresh wild blueberries. For a vegetarian option, try crispy diced fried tempeh.

This is also a great fall or winter salad. Serve it as a lunch with fruit on the side or with a squash soup and bread for an evening meal. This salad is great with fresh sweet corn cut off the cob but can also be made with frozen corn. // **SERVES 6 AS A MAIN COURSE**

1 cup wild rice
½ cup diced red onion
1 stalk celery, diced (½ cup)
3 tablespoons extra-virgin olive oil
1 cup sweet corn, fresh or frozen
¼ cup dried cranberries
2 tablespoons white wine vinegar or apple cider vinegar

½ teaspoon salt
2 teaspoons soy sauce
Pepper
9 to 12 ounces smoked trout, deboned and broken int
    medium-size pieces
Lettuce
Toasted pecans, nectarines, or berries for garnish (optional)

Cook the wild rice, following the directions on the package or in the recipe on page 86.

Sauté the onions and celery in 1 tablespoon of the olive oil for a few minutes; then add the corn and cook a few more minutes until the vegetables are tender. Mix the wild rice, sautéed vegetables, and dried cranberries in a bowl.

In a small bowl, combine the remaining 2 tablespoons of olive oil and the vinegar, salt, soy sauce, and pepper to taste and stir well. Gently fold the dressing into the salad.

Put the lettuce leaves on a platter or individual plates. Spoon the salad onto the lettuce and arrange the trout and any of the optional garnishes you are using on top of the salad.

Cranberry Pear Chutney

This chutney keeps in the fridge for two weeks and adds a sweet and savory component to many meals. We like it with curries or with a simple grain, bean, and vegetable dish. It is also good with chicken, turkey, and pork.

A nice variation is to use diced dried apricots instead of currants or raisins. We much prefer unsulfured apricots: they are not as bright orange, but they have a much better flavor. Some are very caramel-like. // **SERVES 6**

½ tablespoon vegetable oil
1 small onion, diced small
4 to 5 medium pears, diced (3 cups)
½ cup currants or golden raisins
1 tablespoon minced ginger
2 tablespoons lemon juice

3 tablespoons honey
½ teaspoon dried mustard
⅛ teaspoon ground allspice
Pinch of cayenne
2 cups (10 ounces) fresh or frozen cranberries

Heat the vegetable oil in a saucepan. Cook the onions over low heat until they are golden brown and caramelized, about 12 to 15 minutes.

Add the pears, currants, ginger, lemon juice, honey, mustard, allspice, and cayenne and cook over low heat until thoroughly cooked, approximately 15 minutes.

Now add the cranberries for a few minutes, until about half of them pop. Take off the heat.

Serve the chutney at room temperature or cooled.

Arame with Carrots and Sesame

This traditional Japanese dish is served as a side dish along with rice, tofu or fish, and green vegetables. Just a small portion is loaded with iron and minerals. This salad holds well for several days. // **SERVES 4 TO 6**

1 (2-ounce) bag arame
1½ teaspoons vegetable oil
2 tablespoons sesame seeds

2½ tablespoons soy sauce
1 tablespoon water
1 cup julienned carrots

Place the arame in a bowl and cover it with water. Let it soak for 15 minutes, then drain it well.

Heat the oil in a sauté pan and briefly sauté the sesame seeds. As soon as they start to pop, usually only 30 seconds to 1 minute, add the arame; and sauté it for 3 to 4 minutes. Stir in the soy sauce and sauté for another 2 minutes.

Add 1 tablespoon of water, place the carrots on top of the arame, and cover the pan with a lid. Steam the carrots for 1 to 2 minutes. Check for the liquid to be reduced.

Stir to mix carrots in with the arame and let the salad cool.

Arame with Carrots and Sesame

Wakame Cucumber Salad

When buying wakame (a sea vegetable), try to find the kind that is already cut into small pieces. These smaller pieces can be soaked and used as is. If the wakame you buy is dried in its natural form, soak it and then cut small pieces from the large leaf.

Wakame is also very good in soups, especially miso vegetable soup. It is high in antioxidants and minerals. Sea vegetables are good for our blood, supporting the alkalinity our blood should maintain for good health. // **MAKES 2½ CUPS**

Wakame Cucumber Salad

⅓ cup dried wakame, soaked for 15 minutes

1 cucumber

¼ teaspoon salt

2–3 green onions, sliced thinly on a diagonal (2 table-spoons)

⅓ cup rice vinegar

2 tablespoons mirin or 1 teaspoon honey

Drain the soaked wakame.

Cut the cucumber in half lengthwise (scoop out the seeds if they are large); then slice it crosswise into half-moon shapes. Sweat the cucumbers in salt for 5 minutes; then rinse and drain them.

Combine the wakame and cucumber with the green onions, vinegar, and mirin. Chill and serve.

grains, beans,
and vegetables

COOKING RICE AND GRAINS

WHOLE GRAINS are essential for a healthy diet. Today we know that the phytochemicals in whole grains fight against many diseases. Minimally processed grains provide us with oils, vitamins, and fiber that contribute to our well-being.

Brown Rice

Wash 1 cup of brown rice in a saucepan, and drain it. Add ¼ teaspoon of salt and 2½ cups of water. Bring the water to a boil; then turn down the heat and simmer, covered, for 50 minutes. Remove the pan from the heat and let the rice sit, still covered, for 10 more minutes.

To make larger quantities, you need to reduce the ratio of water to rice. (This is true for all whole grains.) For 2 cups of brown rice, add 3½ to 4 cups of water. For 3 cups of brown rice, add 5 cups of water. For 4 cups of brown rice, add 5½ cups of water.

Pressure-cooking brown rice is great. Wash 2 cups of rice. Place it in a pressure cooker with ½ teaspoon of salt and 3½ cups of water. To make a variety of flavors, you can add ½ cup of another whole grain, such as barley, wheat or rye berries, millet, or buckwheat. If you do this, add ½ cup of extra water.

Grains and rice. Top row (left to right): wild rice, basmati rice, brown rice; second row: quinoa, wheat berries, arborio rice; third row: millet, cracked wheat, long-grain brown rice; fourth row: buckwheat, couscous, short-grain brown rice; bottom row: barley, jasmine rice, black rice.

Turn the heat to high, bring the pressure cooker to pressure, and reduce the heat to very low (use a flame diffuser) for 35 minutes. Let the pressure cooker sit to let the pressure subside before opening it.

Make enough rice to have some leftovers, which will allow you to make a few quick dishes in the next two days. Rice patties are a very good way to use pressure-cooked rice, which is a little sticky. It makes a great hot cereal in the morning; bring it to a simmer with water and raisins; then top it with soy rice milk.

You can also add leftover brown rice and a few nuts to smoothies for protein instead of using protein powder. Brown rice is the perfect accompaniment to stir-fry with vegetables and plant protein such as tofu, tempeh, mock duck, or nuts. Add one cup to a pot of soup.

Brown rice has approximately 8 grams of protein per 1 cup serving; it is high in B vitamins and other nutrients. It protects against heart disease and cancers and is calming to the nervous system.

Basmati Rice and Jasmine Rice

Wash 1 cup of rice in a colander. Place the rice in a saucepan with ¼ teaspoon of salt and 1½ cups of water. Bring the water to a boil; then turn down the heat and simmer, covered, for 20 minutes.

Sometimes the simplicity of jasmine rice or basmati rice goes perfectly with a protein dish. Either is nice when cooked along with a sautéed onion and herbs or spices. Ghee and jasmine or basmati rice are always mild and soothing together.

Wild Rice

Wash 1 cup of rice in a colander and place it in a covered saucepan with 1 teaspoon of salt and 3 cups of water.

Bring the water to a boil; then turn down the heat and let the rice simmer for approximately 20 to 50 minutes, depending on the type of rice. Check the package for cooking times, but in general, cook wood-parched, or roasted, lake rice for about 20 minutes and cook typical paddy rice for 50 to 60 minutes.

Wild rice is a hearty food for cold climates. Try a big bowl drizzled with a little soy sauce and olive oil. Wild rice in soups is always a winner.

Make warm pilafs with a few diced vegetables, or serve wild rice cold in a summer salad, lightly dressed in olive oil vinaigrette. Blueberries and corn are nice additions as are celery and nuts.

Wild rice has more protein than other rices. It is rich in minerals and B vitamins.

Quinoa

Thoroughly rinse 1 cup of quinoa in a strainer. Place the quinoa and 2 cups of water in a covered saucepan and bring it to a boil. Reduce to a simmer and cook, covered, until all the water is absorbed, approximately 12 minutes. We like to mix quinoa and rice and cook them together. Try 1 cup of basmati or jasmine rice with ⅓ cup of quinoa. Cook the grains in 2⅓ cups of water with little salt added.

This delicious, quick-cooking grain dates back over five thousand years to the Inca civi-

lization. It is delicious as a side dish, as a hot breakfast cereal, in grain salads, and in soups.

Quinoa has the highest protein content when compared with other grains: 10 grams per 1-cup serving. It contains more calcium than milk does and is also a good source of iron and vitamins B and E.

Buckwheat

Toast 1 cup of dry buckwheat groats in a saucepan over medium heat, stirring constantly, until they are lightly browned. Carefully add 3 cups of water and 1 teaspoon of salt and bring the water to a boil. Turn down the heat and simmer, covered, until all the water is absorbed, approximately 25 minutes.

Cooked buckwheat is one of the most comforting grains in cold weather. Serve a big bowl topped with walnuts and a vegetable stir-fry that includes sliced squash. Or try the Buckwheat Potato Croquettes with Ginger Mushroom Sauce (page 175).

Buckwheat is high in vitamins and minerals and a good source of protein.

Millet

Cook millet just like buckwheat; however, cut the salt down to only ½ teaspoon.

Millet is good mixed with basmati rice (see the recipe on page 85).

You can make a lovely soup, one that is as comforting as chicken soup, with carrots, celery, onions, and some millet. Keep in mind that a little millet goes a long way: it keeps absorbing the liquid, so go easy.

A staple for many Africans, millet is highly alkaline. It is rich in fiber, magnesium, potassium, phosphorus, and vitamin B3. It is a very good source of protein.

Bulgur

Bulgur is available in different grinds, from fine to extra coarse. The medium grind can be cooked in 10 minutes. Add 1 cup of bulgur to 2 cups of salted boiling water. Stir in the bulgur and cook it, covered, for 10 minutes.

Dating back 4,000 years, bulgur wheat is the oldest processed food known to man. During the processing, it is washed, cooked, dried, ground, and sifted to sort it by size. This makes it a healthy quick-cooking grain.

Tabbouleh is a huge favorite as are bulgur-nut salads that include dried apricot or other dried fruits. Use bulgur when making lamb or turkey burgers; it adds great nutritional value, taste, and texture.

In addition to providing fiber and protein, bulgur is rich in B vitamins, iron, phosphorous, and manganese.

Whole Wheat Couscous

Pour 1 cup of couscous and 1 tablespoon of olive oil into boiling salted water. Turn off the heat, cover the pan, and let the couscous sit for 10 minutes. Fluff it with a fork.

Couscous is light and a perfect companion to North African stews. We make pilafs, salads, soups, croquettes, and even cakes with couscous.

The beauty of couscous is you can keep it very simple, yet it is satisfying. Serve it with a side of vegetables or with beans and a little tomato.

Couscous is made with semolina flour. When made from whole wheat semolina, it is a good source of fiber and protein.

COOKING BEANS AND LEGUMES

BEANS AND LEGUMES are known as superfoods. We need to eat more of them, incorporating them into our soups, appetizers, and entrées. The recipes in this section demonstrate that beans and legumes can be simply prepared and can provide the meal's protein. Beans contain more protein than any other plant food and are a great source of fiber, iron, magnesium, potassium, and folate. They contain fats that are good for us and are cholesterol free.

Both canned and dried beans are equally good in most preparations. We have given quantities in cups of cooked beans so you can use either in our recipes. In general, 1 cup of dried beans, chickpeas, or lentils will yield 2 to 3 cups cooked. The time it takes to cook dried beans varies depending on the type of bean, the cooking method, and the soaking time. If salt is a problem for you, it is best not to use canned beans but to cook them from scratch.

Sort through dried beans before cooking them to make sure there are no little stones. Soaking beans shortens their cooking time. It takes about 4 hours for beans to absorb the maximum amount of water they will take in. Cover them with 3 to 4 times their volume of water. If you don't have time for a 4-hour soak, you can cover the beans with boiling water for a quick 1-hour soak.

After the beans have soaked, pour off the soaking water. Put the beans in a pot, cover them with fresh water, and bring it to a boil. Reduce the heat and simmer until the beans are tender. Cooking time will depend on the variety and age of the bean. Most beans will be done in one hour, with the exception of chickpeas, which should always be soaked and will take 1½ hours to cook.

Pressure-cooking beans is a great way to prepare them: they are done so much quicker and have a wonderful plump and creamy texture. If you're in a hurry, the quick-cooking beans are split peas, lentils, black-eyed peas, navy beans, and baby lima beans.

Beans and legumes. Top row (left to right): red lentils, green lentils, green split peas; second row: black chickpeas, navy beans, French lentils; third row: kidney beans, chickpeas, Swedish beans; fourth row: pinto beans, black beans, small red beans; bottom row: black-eyed peas, yellow split peas, cannellini beans.

Brown Rice and Barley Pilaf

This is a simple rice pilaf. Any number of variations can be made to complement your meal or to accommodate what you have in your refrigerator. Parsnips or bell peppers can replace the carrot or celery. Any lightly toasted nut or seed makes a nice garnish on top; try pumpkin seeds, sesame seeds, or pecans. We also often add cooked beans or lentils at the end to make a heartier dish that is rich in protein. // **SERVES 6 TO 8**

1 tablespoon olive oil or vegetable oil
½ cup chopped onion
1 carrot, diced (½ cup)
1 stalk celery, diced (½ cup)
1½ cups short-grain brown rice, rinsed

½ cup pearled barley, rinsed
3½ cups vegetable stock or water
1 teaspoon salt
⅓ cup parsley, chopped
1 tablespoon soy sauce

Heat the oil in a large saucepan. Add the onion and sauté it for a couple of minutes. Add the carrots and celery and cook another 3 minutes. Stir in the brown rice and barley, and then add the stock and salt.

Bring the stock to a boil, cover the pot, and turn down the heat to low. Simmer for 50 to 60 minutes, until the grains are tender and all the liquid has been absorbed.

Gently stir in the parsley and soy sauce.

Buckwheat and Rice Pilaf

Adding buckwheat to a rice pilaf is a good way to increase the nutritional value of the dish. The taste is nutty and delicious. Any leftovers can be eaten as a hot breakfast cereal. Just reheat it with a little water and serve it with any kind of milk. Top it with raisins, nuts, cinnamon, honey, or maple syrup if desired. Leftover brown rice can be treated the same way. // **SERVES 4 TO 6**

¾ cup buckwheat groats
1 cup jasmine rice or another white rice
3¼ cups water
1 teaspoon salt

Dry roast the groats in a frying pan. To do this, heat a pan over medium heat, add the groats, and stir or shake the pan. Roast the grains until they are slightly browned and smell toasty, about 7 minutes. Remove the pan from the heat.

Wash the rice in a strainer until the water is clear.

Buckwheat and Rice Pilaf, Jasmine Rice and Quinoa Pilaf, and Millet with Basmati Rice

Combine the rice, buckwheat groats, water, and salt in a saucepan. Bring the water to a boil over high heat. Cover the pan and reduce the heat. Simmer until all the water is absorbed, approximately 15 minutes. Remove the pan from the heat and let it sit, still covered, for 5 minutes. For added flavor and texture, you can top the grains with sliced green onions, chives, parsley, or nuts.

Wild Rice Pilaf

Wild rice is so delicious you can seriously eat a big bowl of it dressed with just olive oil or butter and soy sauce for dinner and be happy! In the summer, it is great as a grain salad. This is a versatile recipe: add more vegetables or substitute parsnips or squash for the carrot. **// SERVES 6**

¾ cup wild rice
¾ cup brown rice
4 cups water
½ teaspoon salt
1 tablespoon olive oil
1 small onion, chopped

1 large carrot, diced
1 stalk celery, diced
½ cup pecans or walnuts, toasted and coarsely
    chopped (optional)
2 tablespoons chopped parsley
1 tablespoon soy sauce

Rinse the wild rice and the brown rice well. Bring the water to a boil in a saucepan. Add the salt and the rice. Cook slowly, covered, for 45 to 50 minutes, or until the rice is tender.

Heat the olive oil and sauté the onion until it is soft. Add the carrots and celery. Cook for 5 to 8 minutes, stirring occasionally, until the vegetables are softened.

Stir the vegetables into the rice. Add the pecans, parsley, and soy sauce.

WILD RICE //

Wild rice is an aquatic cereal grain that grows wild in shallow lakes and riverbeds, primarily within the North American continent. The wild rice most commonly available in grocery stores is paddy rice. Paddy rice was developed as a farm crop and is cultivated in fields known as paddies. Real wild rice cannot be cultivated because of its specific growth requirements. It is hand harvested in the lakes and rivers of Minnesota and Canada in the fall.

It is important to know what kind of rice you are cooking because the cooking times vary significantly. The long, black, shiny grain is paddy rice, and it takes 50 to 60 minutes to cook. The light-brown, mottled grain has been hand harvested and wood parched. This grain takes only 20 minutes to cook.

Wild rice is done when the grains puff open and are tender. If there is extra water or stock, simply pour it off.

Couscous Pilaf

This dish provides a very simple way to jazz up couscous and makes a very nice side dish for many fish and chicken dishes. Turmeric has health benefits that are widely acknowledged. It is a terrific anti-inflammatory. // **SERVES 4**

2 tablespoons olive oil
½ cup diced red or white onion
1 stalk celery, diced
½ teaspoon turmeric

1 teaspoon ground coriander
1½ cups couscous
1 teaspoon salt
1½ cups boiling water or vegetable stock

Heat the oil in a skillet over medium-high heat. Sauté the onions until they are golden brown, about 3 minutes. Add the celery, turmeric, and coriander and continue to sauté for a few more minutes.

Add the couscous and salt and stir.

Carefully pour in the boiling water, stir, and cover the pan. Turn off the heat and let the couscous sit for about 5 minutes.

Fluff the couscous with a fork before serving it.

Jasmine Rice and Quinoa Pilaf

Quinoa is a light grain that has a natural coating, saponin, on the grain that protects the seed in the field. Usually this is removed before you buy it, but it is best to rinse the grain several times with cold water; you'll need a fine-meshed sieve for this. This pilaf could also be made with basmati rice. The quinoa adds a nice texture to the fragrant jasmine rice and is a terrific source of plant proteins and minerals. // **SERVES 4 TO 6**

Jasmine Rice and Quinoa Pilaf

1½ cups jasmine rice
½ cup quinoa
1 tablespoon olive oil or vegetable oil
½ cup diced onion
1 stalk celery, diced
1 medium carrot, diced
3 cups vegetable stock or water
1 teaspoon salt

Rinse the rice and quinoa well.

Heat the oil in a large saucepan. Add the onions and sauté until soft. Add the celery and carrots. Cook for 2 to 3 minutes.

Add the rice and quinoa. Stir to coat all the grains with the oil and then add the stock and salt.

Cover the pan and bring the stock to a boil. Turn the heat down to low and simmer for 15 minutes.

Remove the pan from the heat and let it sit, still covered, for 5 minutes before serving. The grains should be tender and the liquid fully absorbed.

Millet with Basmati Rice

Millet adds a nice nutty flavor to the basmati rice. The combination makes a mild, comforting dish. Leftovers are good to turn into fried rice or to put in a soup.

Millet, with its high protein content, boosts the nutritional value of the dish and also helps alkalinize our bodies. Consider adding a little turmeric to the water to give the grains a pretty color. We like to incorporate turmeric whenever we can because of its anti-inflammatory effects. // **MAKES 6 CUPS**

½ cup millet
1 cup basmati or jasmine rice

3½ cups water
1 teaspoon salt

Wash the rice and millet in a fine-meshed strainer.

Put the grains, water, and salt in a medium saucepan. Bring the water to a boil, cover the pan, and reduce the heat. Simmer until all the water is absorbed, about 12 to 15 minutes. Let the grains sit, covered, for 5 minutes before serving. If you like, add 1 teaspoon of butter to the pan while the rice is steaming for those last 5 minutes.

Maple–Ginger Red Beans

Better than any baked beans, these red beans are sweet and savory. If you want to add some diced carrots, onions, and celery, simply sauté ½ cup of each in a tablespoon of olive oil for 5 minutes and add the sauté to the beans when you add the rest of the ingredients. // **SERVES 4 TO 6**

1 cup dried small red beans (3 cups cooked) or
    2 (15-ounce) cans, drained and rinsed
2 tablespoons maple syrup

2 tablespoons grated ginger root
1 tablespoon soy sauce
1 teaspoon salt

Soak dried beans for at least two hours, or longer. Drain and rinse the beans.

Put the beans and 3 cups of water in a pot. Cover the pot and bring the water to a boil. Turn down the heat and simmer the beans for 1 hour or until tender. If there is excess liquid, drain off all but ½ cup.

If you are using canned beans or beans cooked earlier, place the beans in a pot and warm them over medium heat for about 10 minutes.

Add the maple syrup, ginger, soy sauce, and salt to the beans. Cook for a couple of minutes longer and serve.

Moroccan Chickpeas with Tomatoes

This lovely chickpea dish goes well with couscous and vegetables. Olives are always a great addition on the side. // **SERVES 4 TO 6**

1 tablespoon olive oil
1 small onion, diced
½ teaspoon cumin
1 teaspoon paprika
¼ teaspoon cinnamon
1 cup crushed or diced tomato

1½ cups cooked chickpeas or 1 (15-ounce) can
   chickpeas, drained and rinsed
¾ cup water or vegetable stock
Salt
2 tablespoons chopped cilantro or parsley

Heat the oil in a pan over medium heat. Sauté the onion in until it is soft. Add the cumin, paprika, and cinnamon. Stir until the spices are toasted and fragrant. Add the tomato, chickpeas, water, and salt. Simmer on low heat for 15 minutes. Add the cilantro just before serving.

Variation

Add 2 cups of chopped fresh spinach during the last 3 minutes.

Moroccan Chickpeas with Tomatoes

Cannellini Beans

This is a bean dish that can be served with a simple pasta with sautéed garlic or alongside a grain with a green vegetable. // **SERVES 4 TO 6**

1 (15-ounce) can cannellini beans or 1½ cups cooked beans
⅓ cup finely diced onion
1 tablespoon olive oil
½ to 1 cup chopped fresh or canned tomato

1 to 2 tablespoons chopped fresh basil or parsley
½ teaspoon salt
Freshly ground pepper

Drain and rinse the beans.

Sauté the onions in the oil until they are soft, about 3 to 4 minutes. Add the beans, tomato, basil, salt, and pepper. Cook over medium heat for about 5 minutes.

Serve as a side dish.

Variations

Add ¼ cup of sliced green olives and ½ cup of diced carrots during the last 5 minutes.

Add 2 cups of kale or spinach cut into 1-inch pieces at the last minute.

Kidney Beans and Green Onions

This is a nearly instant but satisfying dish because of the meaty quality of the kidney beans. Served with a whole grain and a vegetable, these beans are a meal. // **SERVES 3 SIDE OR 2 MAIN PORTIONS**

4 green onions, washed and sliced into rounds
1 tablespoon olive oil
1 (15-ounce) can kidney beans, drained and rinsed
  (or another bean, if you prefer)

1 tablespoon soy sauce
3 to 4 tablespoons water

Sauté the green onions in olive oil for 1 minute. Add the beans, soy sauce, and water. Heat until the water comes to a simmer and the beans are thoroughly heated.

Variation

You can spice up this dish by adding ½ teaspoon of cumin or ginger and a clove of minced garlic to the sauté.

If you would like to add vegetables, try diced carrots, sliced squash, or cabbage, kale, or another green cut into 1-inch pieces. Add the vegetables after you add the beans; they'll need about 5 minutes to cook.

Stewed Lentils

These lentils are delicious with brown rice and a crunchy green salad for a simple dinner that is high in plant-based protein. // **SERVES 4**

1 tablespoon olive oil
½ cup diced red or white onion
1 carrot, diced
1 stalk celery, diced
3 cloves garlic, minced
2 tablespoons tomato paste or 4 tablespoons
    crushed tomatoes

½ teaspoon dried thyme or herbs de Provence (optional)
¾ cup brown or green lentils, rinsed
3¾ cups water
1 tablespoon soy sauce
2 teaspoons Dijon mustard
2 tablespoons chopped fresh parsley or basil

Heat the oil in a medium saucepan. Add the onions, carrots, celery, garlic, tomatoes, and thyme (if using), and sauté for a few minutes. Add the lentils and water. Bring to a boil; then cover and reduce the heat and simmer for 50 to 60 minutes, until the lentils are soft (it's okay if they break down a little). Stir in the soy sauce, mustard, and parsley.

Edamame

It doesn't get much simpler than this. This healthy snack or appetizer takes only three to five minutes to prepare. Children adore popping them out of the pods; adults love them with a beer or a cocktail. Edamame are a great source of plant-based protein and travel well. Pack them in a lunch for a nutritious meal on the go.

Frozen or fresh shelled edamame
Sea salt
Olive oil or toasted sesame oil (optional)

Bring some water to a boil in a saucepan. Add the edamame and cook them for 3 to 5 minutes. After draining the edamame, place them in a bowl and toss them with salt or drizzle on a little olive oil and soy sauce if desired.

Edamame

Edamame and Corn Succotash

When fresh corn is in, it is time to make edamame succotash. This great variation on classic succotash is made with beautiful lime-green, fresh-frozen soybeans. Serve this as part of a summer meal that includes a light grain, such as rice or quinoa, and grilled fish or chicken. // **SERVES 4**

LIME VINAIGRETTE //
1 to 2 cloves garlic, chopped
Grated zest of 1 lime
3 tablespoons fresh lime juice
¼ teaspoon salt
2 tablespoons olive oil

SUCCOTASH //
2 cups shelled frozen edamame
1 tablespoon olive oil
¼ cup chopped sweet red onion
½ cup diced red bell pepper
1 heaping tablespoon finely chopped jalapeño
1 to 2 cups fresh or frozen corn kernels
½ teaspoon salt
Freshly ground pepper
1 tablespoon chopped cilantro or parsley

To make the vinaigrette, combine the garlic, lime zest, lime juice, and salt in a small bowl. Whisk in the olive oil.

Add the edamame to a pot of boiling water. Cook them for 5 minutes after the water returns to a boil. Drain the edamame and place them in a bowl. Pour the vinaigrette over the edamame while they are still warm.

Heat the olive oil in a sauté pan over medium heat. Sauté the onion until it is soft. Add the peppers and cook 2 more minutes. Add the corn, salt, and pepper and cook a few more minutes. Combine the sautéed vegetables with the edamame and the vinaigrette.

Add the cilantro after the salad has come to room temperature.

Braised Kale with Balsamic Vinegar

When you braise food, you begin by sautéing it in a little fat. You then add a little liquid and simmer the dish over a low heat. Braising tenderizes greens while retaining all of their valuable vitamins. **// SERVES 4**

1 bunch kale (¾ pound, about 5 to 6 large leaves)
1 tablespoon olive oil
1 small onion, halved and sliced thin

1 teaspoon soy sauce
1 teaspoon balsamic vinegar

Clean the kale leaves under running water. Remove and discard the stems and any tough ribs. Stack the leaves and cut them into 1-inch strips.

Heat the oil in a large sauté pan. Add the onions and cook until soft. Add the kale and stir, mixing the leaves with the onions and lightly coating the leaves with oil.

Add ¼ cup of water and cover the pan. Reduce the heat and simmer the greens for 5 minutes. Check to see whether you need to add some more liquid. If the pan is dry, add 2 more tablespoons of water. Continue cooking for another 5 minutes. The cooking time will depend on how tender the greens were to start with and how soft you like them. Taste a piece to determine whether you want the kale to cook a little longer. If there is still liquid in the pan when the kale is done, remove the cover and cook it off.

Add the soy sauce and balsamic vinegar. Stir to combine.

GREENS //

Greens are superfoods and help prevent many illnesses and diseases. They are loaded with phytonutrients, iron, minerals, fiber, and vitamins C, K, and A. They are proven to help lower cholesterol.

This large group of leafy green vegetables includes collards, kale, mustard greens, spinach, beet greens, and Swiss chard. Most greens are available year-round in most grocery stores, but you will find the thicker-leaved collards and kale are more tender in the fall after cool weather has set in.

Greens are a great addition to soups and stews and partner well with beans. They are also a delicious and nutritious side dish for any meal. You can interchange different types of greens in any of these recipes; just be aware that some take a little longer to cook than others.

Spinach, Swiss chard, beet greens, and tender young kale leaves can be steamed or blanched and need little besides a good rinsing to prepare. Large kale leaves, collards, and mustard greens are often best with the tough ribs of the leaf removed. Simply cut along each side of the stem with the knife slightly angled. You can cook the stems (they will take a little longer to cook) or discard them, but they are delicious!

Kale is more tender and flavorful after cool weather arrives.

All greens require a good washing. Rinse off each leaf or fill a sink or bowl with cool water and swirl the greens around. Lift the greens out and repeat until the water is free of dirt or sand.

Swiss Chard with Garlic and Red Pepper Flakes

Swiss chard is very nutritious and available year-round. This recipe is an easy way to spice it up. (The recipe also works well with kale.) You can increase or decrease the heat by changing the quantity of red pepper. Chard bunches look quite large but cook down to a smaller quantity than you might expect. One pound of whole chard leaves yields about 5 to 6 packed cups of chopped leaves, which cook down to two or three servings. // SERVES 2 TO 3

1 bunch Swiss chard
1 tablespoon olive oil
3 cloves garlic, chopped
Pinch of crushed red pepper

Salt and pepper
⅓ cup water
1 teaspoon red wine vinegar or lemon juice

Cut the leaves from the stems. Wash the leaves well, and then coarsely chop them. You can use the stems as well if you like. Simply slice them on the diagonal and sauté them along with the garlic. They will take a few minutes longer to cook than the leaves.

Heat the oil in a sauté pan. Briefly sauté the garlic, and then add the crushed red pepper. Add the Swiss chard, stirring to combine the leaves with the garlic and red pepper. Add a little salt and pepper and the water.

Cover the pan and simmer for 5 minutes over medium-high heat. Remove the lid and continue cooking until the liquid is gone. If the liquid is gone and greens seem not quite done, you may need to add a splash more water.

Sprinkle the greens with the vinegar and serve.

Braised Yams, Onions, and Broccoli

Cooking a few vegetables together can make a very simple meal perfectly delicious. Serve these vegetables with a simple grain on the side. To add more protein, combine some tempeh or tofu with the vegetables. When the garden is full of fresh herbs, try substituting some chopped herbs for the ginger. // **SERVES 4 TO 6**

2 tablespoons olive oil
2 medium onions, quartered lengthwise (leave some of
    the root to hold the onion quarters together)
2 yams, peeled and cut into ½-inch rounds

½ tablespoon chopped ginger
1 tablespoon soy sauce
½ cup water
2 cups broccoli florets

Heat the olive oil in a large skillet over medium heat. Add the onions and yams. Do not stir until they become golden brown on one side, about 3 to 5 minutes.

Once the onions and yams are browned on one side, stir them and add the ginger, soy sauce, and water. Cover the pan and simmer for about 10 minutes, until the yams are tender.

Add the broccoli, cover the pan again, and cook for another 3 minutes. Check the broccoli. You should be able to just pierce the stem with a fork, but the color should still be bright green. If the broccoli is not done, cover the pan again and check every few minutes until it is done. If all the water cooks off, simply add a little more.

Variation

Substitute kale, green beans, or cauliflower for the broccoli.

Cabbage with Fennel Seeds

Cabbage is so overlooked when it comes to delicious and nutritious vegetables. Cabbage is loaded with phytonutrients and protects against many diseases. It keeps so well that you can still buy local cabbage months after winter sets in. Chef Nick Schneider taught us this comforting, simple dish. **// SERVES 4**

2 tablespoons butter
1 teaspoon fennel seeds
1 teaspoon mustard seeds
¼ teaspoon salt

1 clove garlic, sliced
1 pound (½ medium head) cabbage, cored and sliced thin
¼ cup water

Melt the butter in a large sauté pan. Add the fennel and mustard seeds, salt, and garlic and sauté for 30 seconds to 1 minute. Add the shredded cabbage. Stir to combine.

Add the water, cover the pan, and steam for 6 to 7 minutes. The water should be reduced. If it is not, cook another minute or two with the lid off.

Serve warm.

Variations

Use olive oil instead of butter.

Combine red and green cabbage.

Place julienned carrots or green beans on top of the cabbage while you steam it.

Braised Broccoli and Garlic

Organic broccoli has such a delicious flavor when simply braised with a little garlic and olive oil. The trick is to add just a splash of water to finish cooking it. **// SERVES 4 TO 6**

1 bunch broccoli
1 tablespoon olive oil
4 to 5 large garlic cloves, sliced thinly

Salt
Pepper
Lemon juice or vinegar, for serving

Cut the broccoli heads from the stems. Peel and slice the stems, and cut the heads into large florets.

Heat the oil in a sauté pan, add the garlic, and lightly brown it. Add the broccoli and sauté for another minute.

Add 3 to 4 tablespoons of water, cover the pan, and simmer over medium-high heat. Check the broccoli for doneness after 4 to 5 minutes. The broccoli is done when a fork easily pierces the stem. The broccoli should still be firm and dark green. If the water is gone before the broccoli is cooked, add another tablespoon of water.

Remove from the heat and serve with a squeeze of lemon juice or a splash of good vinegar.

Stovetop Caramelized Onions and Squash

Some winter squash peels are perfectly edible, in which case you don't even need to peel the squash for this dish. If the skin is tough, you can easily cut it off as you eat or you can peel the squash before you cook it—either way works. **// SERVES 4 TO 6**

1 tablespoon olive oil
2 large onions, quartered lengthwise (leave some of the
    root so the onion quarters don't fall apart)
1 medium-size winter squash, cut into 1- to 2-inch cubes
    (3 to 5 cups)

1 tablespoon soy sauce
⅓ cup water

Heat the oil in a skillet and sauté the onions for a few minutes over medium to high heat until browned on one side.

Turn the onions over and add the squash, soy sauce, and water. Bring the liquid to a boil, cover the skillet, and turn the heat down to medium-low. Cook for approximately 15 minutes.

Variations

Add about a tablespoon of minced ginger when you sauté the onions. Add a green vegetable, such as cabbage, kale, collards, green beans, or broccoli, for the last 5 minutes of cooking.

GRAINS, BEANS, AND VEGETABLES

NISTLER FARMS //

Jeff Nistler of Nistler Farms in Maple Plain is a regular vendor at the Mill City Farmers Market, where people line up to buy his amazing fresh-picked sweet corn. The stand can get so busy that he will often have to resupply it several times during the day. Like all great sweet corn, it's even good uncooked, a sure sign of freshness and a good indication that you don't need to cook it very long. Jeff hands out free samples of uncooked corn at the market to prove the point.

Spoonriver buys Nistler's sweet corn by the gunnysack when it's in season. For us, it's a two-person job just to get the bag across the plaza from the market to the restaurant. When the corn finally runs out for the season, Nistler Farms also has a wonderful selection of squashes, melons, and pumpkins.

Baked Winter Squash

Winter squash lends itself to being prepared many different ways. Most of us are familiar with acorn squash halved and baked with butter and brown sugar in the cavity. Now there are so many more varieties in the markets: butternut, kabocha, buttercup, sweet dumpling, and delicata, to name a few. You can cut up squash and put it in soups, stews, and stir-fries, or serve it steamed or braised or baked. Here we offer a simple glaze to put on squash slices before baking them. You can use this glaze on root vegetables as well. // **SERVES 4 TO 6**

1 tablespoon sunflower or safflower oil
1 tablespoon maple syrup
1 tablespoon soy sauce
1 medium winter squash

Place the oil, maple syrup, and soy sauce in a small bowl and whisk to combine. There will be enough glaze for one medium squash. If you are baking a large squash, you may want to double the amount of glaze.

Preheat the oven to 375 degrees and lightly oil a sheet pan.

Winter squash, curing before going to market

You can peel the squash or leave the skin on. Cut the squash in half and clean out the seeds. Cut the squash into thick slices, one inch or more. Brush the glaze onto both sides of the slices and place them on the sheet pan.

Bake until the squash is tender. Some varieties may be done in 20 minutes; others may take up to 45 minutes.

Parsnips and Yams

This is a colorful, elegant, and comforting way to prepare root vegetables. Cooking them on top of the stove is a much quicker and lighter method than roasting them for an hour in olive oil. // **SERVES 4 TO 6**

3 medium parsnips, cut into ¼-inch cubes (2 cups)
1 large yam, cut into 1-inch cubes (2 cups)
¼ cup orange juice
¼ cup water

½ teaspoon sea salt
Pepper
1 to 2 tablespoons extra-virgin olive oil

Place the parsnips and yams in a medium skillet with the orange juice, water, salt, and pepper. Cover and cook over medium-high heat until the vegetables are just tender and all the liquid has been absorbed, approximately 10 to 12 minutes. Add a bit more water if needed to keep the vegetables from sticking.

Toss with olive oil before serving.

Variation

Add 2 teaspoons of minced ginger for the last few minutes of cooking.

Roasted Potatoes

Look for organic and farm-fresh potatoes at your local farmers' market, where many interesting varieties are now available. Prepared this way, they are sweet and almost like candy. **// SERVES 4**

1½ pounds potatoes (about 3 large russets or 4 medium
    yellow or red potatoes)
1 tablespoon olive oil
½ teaspoon salt
2 tablespoons chopped fresh rosemary
Freshly ground pepper

Preheat the oven to 450 degrees.

You can peel the potatoes or leave the skin on. Cut the potatoes into wedges or large chunks. Toss the potatoes with olive oil, and then add the salt, rosemary, and pepper to taste. Toss again to distribute the seasonings.

Spread the potatoes on a baking sheet. Roast them for 20 minutes. Loosen and turn the potatoes; then roast another 10 to 15 minutes, until they are golden brown. Serve immediately.

A mix of red, yellow, and blue potatoes captivates the eye as well as the taste buds.

entrée

East Indian Curry with Red Lentils

In fall and early winter, when winter squash and cauliflower are in the markets, this spicy stew is a favorite. You can easily alter the recipe to increase or decrease the heat. You may also want to change the vegetables, depending on what is in season. During the summer, try pea pods and carrots or spinach and sweet potatoes. // **SERVES 6 TO 8**

½ cup red lentils
1 tablespoon olive oil or vegetable oil
1 large onion, cut into large pieces
1 red bell pepper, diced large (1 cup)
4 cups diced winter squash or carrots
1½ cups diced fresh tomato or 1 (15-ounce) can diced
    or crushed tomato
3 cups vegetable stock

1½ teaspoons salt
1 (14-ounce) can light coconut milk
2 to 3 tablespoons red curry paste
3 cups cauliflower florets (1-inch pieces)
2½ cups green beans or snap peas, cut into 2-inch pieces
2 cups basmati rice
Fresh cilantro (optional)

Sort through the lentils to make sure there are no stones. Place the lentils in a bowl and rinse them several times with water. Put the lentils and 3 cups of water in a small saucepan. Bring the water to a boil; then turn down the heat and simmer, uncovered, until the lentils are soft, about 15 minutes.

Heat the oil in a large soup pot. Sauté the onion over medium heat until it is soft. Add the peppers, squash, tomatoes, stock, and salt and stir. Simmer until the squash is tender, approximately 10 to 12 minutes.

Place a few tablespoons of coconut milk in a small bowl and stir in the red curry paste. Add this mixture to the stew. Add the rest of the coconut milk along with the cauliflower and green beans. Bring the stew to a low boil; then turn down the heat, stir in the lentils, and simmer for 5 minutes.

Meanwhile, prepare the rice. Rinse the rice until the water is clear. Combine the rice and 3 cups of water in a saucepan with 1 teaspoon salt. Bring the water to a boil; then simmer the rice, covered, over low heat for 12 minutes. Turn off the heat and let the rice sit, still covered, for five minutes before serving it.

Serve the stew with the rice, and garnish it with cilantro.

East Indian Curry with Red Lentils

Butternut Squash, Vegetable, and White Bean Gratin

When fall comes, this is one of the first meals we make. We're fortunate to have a good farmers' market where we can fill up the trunk with a variety of squash from one of our favorite growers. This gratin is nice served with wild rice and a very simple green salad. // **SERVES 6**

1 medium butternut squash
2 tablespoons olive oil
6 cloves garlic, minced
2 cups leeks, cut in half and sliced
1 red bell pepper, julienned
3 cups mushrooms (wild, if available), sliced
1½ tablespoons butter
1 (15-ounce) can white beans, drained and rinsed

4 tomatoes, sliced
¼ cup chopped herbs (any mixture of basil, marjoram, parsley, rosemary, thyme, mint, sage)
½ teaspoon salt
½ teaspoon pepper
¾ cup roasted walnuts
1 cup grated Gruyère cheese

Preheat the oven to 375 degrees.

Peel the squash, remove the seeds, and slice it into ¼- to ½-inch strips. Lightly brush the squash with ½ tablespoon of the olive oil, sprinkle on some salt and pepper, and bake on a sheet pan until tender, about 15 minutes.

Heat the remaining 1½ tablespoons of olive oil in a skillet and sauté the garlic, leeks, and red bell pepper for 5 minutes. Scrape the sauté into a bowl and set it aside. Melt the butter in the pan and sauté the mushrooms for 5 minutes, or until golden brown, stirring frequently. Salt them lightly and set them aside.

Reduce the oven temperature to 350 degrees. In a 9 × 13-inch baking dish, layer the ingredients in the following order: squash, mushrooms, white beans, leek and pepper mixture, tomatoes, herbs, salt and pepper, walnuts, and cheese.

Cover the dish with foil and bake for 30 minutes. Remove the foil and bake 10 minutes longer.

Couscous Platter with Grilled Vegetables

This is a great dish for entertaining because the sky is the limit for how many people you can serve. Consider serving the couscous and vegetables with harissa and lamb or chicken kebabs (page 145). **// SERVES 6**

1 eggplant
1 zucchini
1 sweet red bell pepper
1 red onion
½ pound green beans, blanched
Olive oil
Salt and pepper
2¼ cups water
2 cups couscous
1 (15-ounce) can chickpeas, drained and rinsed
1 bunch parsley, chopped
1 bunch mint, chopped

GARNISH OPTIONS//
Olives
Pistachios or almonds
Golden raisins or sliced apricots
Feta cheese or goat cheese
Cilantro sprigs

Preheat the oven to 400 degrees or prepare the grill.

Slice the eggplant into ½-inch rounds and brush on a generous amount of olive oil, sprinkle with salt and pepper, and place the eggplant on a sheet pan. Roast the eggplant until it is golden brown and soft, about 20 minutes. Do not be afraid of overcooking eggplant; undercooked eggplant is firm and not very tasty. If you are grilling, avoid high heat.

A quick dip in an ice bath after blanching stops the cooking.

The zucchini, red pepper, and red onion can be grilled or roasted as well. Cut the vegetables in large, thick slices or wedges. How you cut the onion does not matter much if you are roasting, but if you are grilling, cut the onion lengthwise into wedges, leaving part of the stem end remaining so the onions do not fall apart and slip through the grill grate. Brush the vegetables with oil, and roast or grill until just tender.

Bring the water and salt to a boil. Add the couscous, stir, place the chickpeas on top of the couscous, and turn the heat off. Cover the pan and let it sit for 10 minutes. Fluff the couscous with a fork.

Add the parsley and mint and toss to mix in the herbs and chickpeas. Place the couscous on a large platter and arrange the grilled vegetables and blanched green beans around it. Garnish with olives, nuts, fruit, cheese, and cilantro.

Broccoli and Winter Squash Sauté over Couscous

This quick vegetable sauté makes an easy dinner when served with couscous or rice. You could use cauliflower or green beans in place of the broccoli and substitute carrots for the winter squash.
// SERVES 4 TO 6

VEGETABLE SAUTÉ //
2 to 3 tablespoons olive oil
1 onion, chopped
2 garlic cloves, sliced
1 small winter squash, peeled, seeded, and cut into
    ¼-inch slices (about 2 cups)
1 cup water
1 (15-ounce) can chickpeas, drained
1 large tomato, diced, or ¾ cup canned diced or
    crushed tomato
2 tablespoons soy sauce
½ teaspoon salt
1½ teaspoons dried thyme or 2 teaspoons chopped
    fresh thyme
2 teaspoons coriander
2½ cups broccoli florets (1 bunch broccoli)

COUSCOUS //
1¾ cups water
1 teaspoon salt
1½ cups couscous
1 tablespoon olive oil

Heat the olive oil in a large sauté pan. Sauté the onion for 3 minutes. Add the garlic and cook for another minute. Add the squash and continue cooking for another 3 to 4 minutes over medium heat, stirring gently if the squash is browning.

Add the water, chickpeas, tomatoes, soy sauce, salt, thyme, and coriander. Cover the pan and simmer over low heat until the squash is tender, approximately 5 minutes.

Stir in the broccoli and cover the pan again. Cook another 3 to 4 minutes, until the broccoli is just tender enough to pierce with a fork. Do not overcook the broccoli. It should still be bright green and firm.

Meanwhile, bring the water and salt for the couscous to a boil in a small saucepan. Add the couscous and the olive oil; stir, turn off the heat, and cover the pan tightly. Let the couscous sit for 7 minutes. Fluff before serving.

Serve the sautéed vegetables over the couscous.

Broccoli and Winter Squash Sauté over Couscous

Broccoli and Potato Vegetable Pie

The eggs in this tart might make you think that this is only for brunch, but served with a big green salad, it's great for any meal. It's also great for entertaining because your preparation is done in advance. // **SERVES 6 TO 8**

ENTRÉES

2 medium potatoes, sliced ¼ to ⅓ inch thick
1 tablespoon olive oil
1½ cups broccoli florets
3 green onions, chopped
3 eggs
½ cup cream
1 teaspoon fresh herbs, such as thyme, marjoram,
    or whatever your favorite is

1 teaspoon salt
Pepper
½ cup Swiss or Gruyère cheese
⅓ cup pitted black olives
1 prebaked 9-inch tart or pie shell (page 233)

Preheat the oven to 375 degrees.

Cook the potatoes in a small pan of gently boiling water until they are tender but not breaking up, about 12 minutes. Drain the potatoes and set them aside.

Heat the olive oil in a skillet and cook the broccoli and green onions for a few minutes with ¼ cup water.

In a small bowl, whisk together the eggs, cream, herbs, salt, and pepper. Stir the broccoli and the olives into the egg mixture.

Put the cheese on the bottom of the shell. Layer the potato slices over the cheese. Then pour the egg mixture over top.

Bake the tart for 30 minutes. The tart will be set and lightly brown.

Garnish with cherry tomatoes.

Provence Vegetable Tart

We love this tart with anchovies on top. If anchovies don't appeal, certainly some olives are a must. The tart is best served with a spinach and chickpea salad. **// SERVES 6 TO 8**

1 prebaked 9-inch tart or pie shell (page 233)
1 small to medium eggplant
3 tablespoons olive oil
1 small onion, diced small
½ teaspoon salt
Pepper
1 large tomato, diced, or 1 cup canned diced tomatoes
¼ teaspoon dried oregano
2 eggs
½ cup cream, milk, or grain milk
1 to 2 tablespoons coarsely grated Parmesan cheese
2 tablespoons finely sliced fresh basil
Anchovy fillets (optional)
Green or black olives

Preheat the oven to 375 degrees.

Peel the eggplant and cut it into half-inch cubes.

Heat the olive oil in a large skillet. Sauté the eggplant over medium heat, stirring occasionally, until it is browned on all sides. Add the onions and season with salt and pepper. Continue cooking until the onions have softened.

Add the tomatoes and oregano. Simmer gently, stirring occasionally, until the mixture has thickened and the eggplant is soft. Turn off the heat and let the vegetables cool for a few minutes.

Freshness that's worth every penny.

In a small bowl, whisk together the eggs and cream. Add the cheese and basil. Stir the cooled vegetables into the egg mixture.

Spoon the filling into the shell. Garnish the top with flat anchovy fillets or salty black or green olives before baking.

Bake for 30 minutes. The tart will be set and lightly browned.

Italian Pistou

This is a very versatile vegetable soup that you serve topped with a fresh pesto. Use whatever vegetables you have. You could substitute sweet potato for the squash or kale for the green beans. This is easily a whole meal when served with bread and a simple olive spread. // **SERVES 6 TO 8**

SOUP//

2 tablespoons olive oil

1 onion, diced

4 to 6 cloves garlic, minced

1 small butternut squash, peeled and cut into 1-inch cubes (1 cup)

1 red bell pepper, diced

1 cup green beans, cut into 1-inch pieces

1 (15-ounce) can diced tomatoes

1 (15-ounce) can cannellini beans, drained and rinsed

1 teaspoon salt

Freshly ground pepper

10 cups vegetable stock

1 zucchini or summer squash, diced

½ pound tube-shaped pasta, cooked

PESTO//

2 cups slightly packed basil (or substitute arugula, spinach, or parsley)

4 cloves garlic

2 tablespoons pine nuts (or pistachios, almonds, or sunflower seeds)

½ cup olive oil

1 teaspoon salt

½ cup grated Parmesan

Heat the olive oil in a soup pot. Sauté the onion for 2 to 3 minutes. Add the garlic and cook another minute. Add the squash, red pepper, and green beans. Continue cooking for about 5 minutes.

Add the tomatoes, cannellini beans, salt, pepper, and stock. Bring the stock to a boil; then turn it down to a simmer. Simmer until the vegetables are just tender, about 4 to 5 minutes.

Add the zucchini and cook another minute, and then remove the pot from the heat.

To make the pesto, place the basil, garlic, pine nuts, oil, and salt in a blender or a food processor. Process until the pesto is smooth. Stir in the cheese.

Place some pasta in the bottom of each bowl and ladle soup over top. Place one large spoonful of pesto on top of each bowl of soup when serving.

Roasted Winter Vegetable Stew

Serve this comforting stew with a fresh, crunchy green salad and a crusty loaf of bread. If you prefer to add cooked chicken instead of beans, that will work quite well. // **SERVES 4 TO 6**

STEW VEGETABLES //

1 medium onion, cut into large dice

1 rutabaga or 2 to 3 parsnips, cut into ½-inch pieces
    (2 cups)

1 stalk celery, thickly sliced

1 red bell pepper, cut into 1½- to 2-inch pieces

3 carrots, cut into 1½- to 2-inch pieces

4 small red or yellow potatoes, cut into 1½- to 2-inch pieces

3 tablespoons olive oil

2 tablespoons water

8 ounces mushrooms, halved or left whole if small

1 (15-ounce) can large kidney beans, drained and rinsed

SAUCE //

3 tablespoons olive oil

3 tablespoons flour

½ teaspoon dried thyme

½ teaspoon fennel seeds

1 bay leaf

2½ cups vegetable stock or chicken stock

½ teaspoon salt

Freshly ground pepper

Preheat the oven to 450 degrees.

Toss the onion, rutabagas, celery, red bell pepper, carrots, and potatoes with 2 tablespoons of the olive oil; then place them in a large roasting pan and add the water.

Roast the vegetables for 45 minutes to 1 hour, or until they are nicely browned and tender when pierced with a fork. Stir the vegetables twice while they are roasting.

Meanwhile, prepare the sauce. Heat the oil in a small saucepan. Add the flour, whisking to combine. Continue stirring the roux as the flour cooks. After a few minutes, the roux will start to smell slightly toasted or nutty and turn light brown. Add the thyme, fennel seeds, bay leaf, salt, and pepper. Add the stock slowly while whisking. Continue stirring until the stock comes to a low boil and thickens. Remove the sauce from the heat.

Reduce the oven temperature to 350 degrees.

Sauté the mushrooms in the remaining 1 tablespoon of olive oil for about 5 to 7 minutes. Add the mushrooms to the pan of roasted vegetables, stir in the beans and the sauce, and cover the pan.

Bake, covered, for 20 minutes.

LOON ORGANICS //

Laura Frerichs and Adam Cullip started Loon Organics in 2005 as a two-acre incubator farm at Gardens of Eagan in Farmington. By 2008, they had moved to their new farm in Hutchinson, where they grow eight acres of certified organic vegetables and herbs. We think people like Laura and Adam are the future of farming. They are committed, hardworking, and just incredible people.

Loon Organics is one of the most successful vendors at the Mill City Farmers Market. Market visitors just love their produce. They supply Spoonriver with a wide variety of amazing greens, multicolored carrots, lettuces, romanesco, tomatoes, cauliflower, and celery root.

Adam Cullip (center) and Laura Frerichs (right) of Loon Organics, Hutchinson, Minnesota

Baby Lima Beans with Polenta

Serve this simple lima bean dish with either polenta or brown rice and a green vegetable or a salad. It is delicious the second day and can easily be turned into a completely different meal by combining the beans with a short tube pasta and some kale or another type of green. // **SERVES 4**

BEANS //

1½ cups baby lima beans

6 cups water

1 (15-ounce) can diced tomatoes or 1½ cups chopped
    fresh tomatoes

1 medium onion, diced

1 large carrot, diced

½ cup green olives (optional)

1½ teaspoons rosemary, chopped if fresh

1 teaspoon paprika

½ teaspoon salt

POLENTA //

4 cups water

1 cup polenta or coarse-ground cornmeal

1 teaspoon salt

1½ cups grated Parmesan cheese (optional)

Olive oil (optional)

Clean the lima beans and place them in a saucepan with the water. Bring the water to a boil; then turn down the heat and simmer the beans, uncovered, for 20 minutes. Skim off any foam.

Add the tomatoes, onions, carrots, olives (if using), rosemary, paprika, and salt and bring the water back to a boil. Turn down the heat and simmer, covered, for approximately 30 minutes, or until the beans are soft. Some of the beans may fall apart, creating a creamy sauce.

Meanwhile, make the polenta. Bring the water to a boil. Add the salt and then pour in the polenta in a slow, steady stream, stirring with a whisk so you do not get clumps.

Turn down the heat to a simmer and stir well. Cover the pan and continue cooking, stirring frequently, until the polenta is thick and creamy, about 30 to 60 minutes. The coarser the cornmeal, the longer you want to cook it.

At this point, you can serve the polenta as is or you can add ½ cup of grated Parmesan cheese, some olive oil, or both.

If you prefer grilled or broiled polenta, pour the cooked polenta onto a greased sheet pan and smooth it with a spatula. You want it to be about ½ inch thick. Let it cool for 15 minutes or longer, until it is firm. Cut the polenta into the shape you want and brush both sides with olive oil. Grill or broil until browned on both sides.

Serve the beans over the polenta.

Sweet Corn, Rice, and Pumpkin Seed Loaf

Try serving this topped with an avocado sour cream, alongside a green salad with mango slices and the simple kidney bean recipe (page 101). You could substitute black beans or pintos in that recipe.
// **SERVES 6 TO 7**

1 cup short-grain brown rice
½ cup pumpkin seeds
1 medium-large onion, diced small
1 tablespoon chopped garlic
2 tablespoons olive oil
1 stalk celery, diced small
1½ cups corn (frozen is fine)
¼ teaspoon turmeric
2 teaspoons coriander

2 eggs
1 cup grated cheddar or your favorite cheese
½ cup dry bread crumbs
2 tablespoons chopped parsley
Juice of 1 orange
1 teaspoon salt
½ teaspoon pepper
⅛ teaspoon cayenne

Preheat the oven to 350 degrees and oil a loaf pan.

Add the rice to 2½ cups of salted water. Bring it to a boil, turn down the heat, cover the pot, and cook approximately 45 minutes over low heat.

Spread the pumpkin seeds on a baking sheet and roast them in the oven for 10 minutes. Coarsely chop the seeds.

Sauté the onions and garlic in the olive oil for 3 to 5 minutes. Add the celery and continue sautéing for 2 more minutes. Now add the corn, turmeric, and coriander and sauté for another 2 minutes. Turn off the heat and let the mixture cool.

In a large bowl, mix together the cooked rice, roasted pumpkin seeds, and sautéed vegetables. Stir in the eggs, cheese, bread crumbs, parsley, orange juice, salt, pepper, and cayenne. (Make sure the mixture has cooled somewhat before adding the eggs; you don't want the egg to curdle.) Put the mixture into the loaf pan and cover it with aluminum foil.

Bake for 45 minutes, uncover the pan, and bake for an additional 30 minutes. Let the loaf sit for 15 minutes before serving.

Squash Risotto

Risotto has endless possibilities. On its own, it can be a great side dish with fish or poultry. Add vegetables, top it with nuts, and you have a main course. Try whatever is in season, adding the cooked vegetables when the rice has nearly finished cooking. Risotto that pairs asparagus with lemon zest or peas with parsley is nice in the spring. Here, we have a great fall and winter risotto made with winter squash. The directions call for cooking the squash on top of the stove, but you could also roast the squash in the oven. Risotto should be slightly al dente and creamy. You want it loose enough that it runs a little on the plate. // SERVES 6

7 to 8 cups vegetable stock
1 medium winter squash, cut into 1-inch pieces (4 cups)
3 tablespoons olive oil
1 medium onion or leek, diced
2 tablespoons minced garlic
2 cups Arborio rice
½ cup white wine

¼ teaspoon dried sage
2 tablespoons chopped fresh basil
Pinch of nutmeg
Salt and pepper
¼ to ⅓ cup grated Parmesan cheese
Roasted pine nuts or walnuts

Put the stock into a saucepan and place it over medium-low heat. Keep the stock simmering while you make the risotto. You want the stock to be hot as you add it to the cooking rice.

Sauté the squash in 1 tablespoon of the olive oil over medium heat until it is just tender, about 10 minutes. If the squash starts to stick to the pan, add a few tablespoons of the stock and cover the pan for a few minutes. Salt the squash and set it aside, uncovered.

In a heavy-bottomed pan, heat the remaining 2 tablespoons of olive oil. Sauté the onions and garlic for 3 minutes. Add the rice, stirring to coat the grains with oil. Add the wine and cook, stirring, until the wine has been absorbed.

Begin adding the simmering stock. Add 1 cup of stock and stir. Keep the temperature high enough to maintain a good simmer. As the stock is absorbed, continue adding stock one cup at a time. Stir continually.

When the rice is almost done and only two more additions of stock remain, add the squash, sage, basil, and nutmeg. Add another cup of stock and stir well. When this stock has been absorbed, taste the rice. It should have a little bite to it, chewy but tender. Season with salt and pepper to taste. The risotto should be pourable but not thin. If it is too thick, add a little more liquid; if it is too thin, continue cooking until it thickens. Add the cheese and stir well.

Serve right away topped with roasted pine nuts or walnuts.

Mock Duck Sloppy Janes

This is a scrumptious vegetarian variation on the traditional Joe. **// SERVES 4 TO 5**

1 onion, diced
½ cup diced green or red bell pepper
1 stalk celery, diced
1 tablespoon minced garlic
2 tablespoons olive oil
1 (8-ounce) package mock duck (seitan) or tempeh, minced
1 teaspoon oregano
⅛ teaspoon ginger

1½ teaspoons chili powder
3 tablespoons tomato paste mixed into ¾ cup water
1 teaspoon dry mustard or Dijon mustard
2 tablespoons soy sauce
1 tablespoon honey or sugar
1 tablespoon vinegar
1 tablespoon molasses
Salt and pepper

Sauté the onions, peppers, celery, and garlic in the olive oil for approximately 3 to 4 minutes. Add the mock duck, oregano, ginger, and chili powder and sauté a few more minutes.

Add the tomato paste, mustard, soy sauce, honey, vinegar, and molasses, and simmer for a few more minutes. Season with salt and pepper to taste.

Serve the sloppy Janes on buns or large rolls. Avoid buns that are too heavy; a light whole wheat bun is best.

Mock Duck Tacos

Mock duck, or seitan, is made from wheat gluten, not soy, and was developed by vegetarian Buddhist monks in ancient China. This plant-based protein is a very nutritious alternative to meat. A pot of brown rice and a salad, plus your favorite salsa, are nice accompaniments. // **SERVES 6 TO 8**

1 medium onion, chopped
1 red or green bell pepper, diced medium-small
1 or 2 jalapeños, chopped
2 tablespoons vegetable oil or olive oil
2 cloves garlic, minced
1 tablespoon chili powder
1 (8-ounce) package mock duck (seitan), traditionally
    seasoned, squeezed to remove liquid, and chopped small

Juice of half a lime
3 tablespoons soy sauce
Pinch of salt
12 to 16 corn tortillas
Grated cheese

Sauté the onions and peppers in the oil for 5 minutes. Add the garlic and chili powder and cook, stirring, for a few more minutes. Add the mock duck, lime juice, and soy sauce.

Cook over medium heat, stirring often, until the mixture is heated through. Season with salt to taste.

Preheat the oven to 400 degrees.

We like to make these tacos open-faced and bake them in the oven on a sheet pan. Brush both sides of each tortilla with olive oil or vegetable oil and place it on the pan. Top each tortilla with about 3 tablespoons of the taco filling and sprinkle on some grated cheese.

Bake until the tortillas are crispy on the bottom, about 8 minutes. Serve with your favorite salsa.

Mushroom Tempeh Stroganoff

Tempeh is a plant-based protein made from fermented soybeans and grains. It has a rich and nutty character and is a great addition to many dishes, such as stir-fries, pasta sauces, and croquettes.

// SERVES 6 TO 8

TEMPEH//
2 tablespoons olive oil
1 tablespoon soy sauce
2 teaspoons finely minced garlic
2 (8-ounce) cakes tempeh, cubed

SAUCE//
1 large onion, chopped
7 tablespoons olive oil
6 cloves garlic, minced
1 carrot, diced
1 stalk celery, diced
1 red or yellow bell pepper, diced

1½ pounds assorted mushrooms, cleaned and sliced
4 tablespoons flour
3 cups vegetable stock
¾ cup red wine
2 tablespoons tomato paste
2 teaspoons dried thyme
⅛ to ¼ teaspoon cayenne
½ teaspoon dried marjoram
½ teaspoon salt
Pepper
Fettuccine pasta, for serving
Fresh dill–sour cream, for garnish

Preheat the oven to 400 degrees.

Stir together the olive oil, soy sauce, and garlic. Toss the cubed tempeh in the marinade.

Bake the tempeh until it is until golden brown, approximately 12 minutes. Set it aside.

Sauté the onions in 1 tablespoon of the oil until soft. Add the garlic, carrots, celery, and peppers and sauté until tender, approximately 5 more minutes. Reserve.

In a large skillet, sauté the mushrooms in 2 more tablespoons of the olive oil over high heat until they brown. You may need to sauté the mushrooms in two batches so they brown rather than sweat in their own juices. Reserve.

In a large pot, heat the remaining 4 tablespoons of oil; then add the flour, mixing well, to make a roux. Continue to cook the roux until the flour smells nutty and is golden brown in color.

In another pan, heat the stock, wine, tomato paste, thyme, cayenne, and marjoram, and then whisk this mixture into the roux. Make sure to stir quickly to avoid any lumps. Add the salt and pepper. Simmer the sauce for a few minutes and then add the sautéed mushrooms and vegetables.

Serve the tempeh and the sauce over fettuccine noodles. Garnish the stroganoff with fresh dill–sour cream.

Tomato Porcini Sauce with Chicken and Pasta

Dried mushrooms make this dish special. They add a rich, earthy flavor. Serve the sauce with a rustic pasta, such as rigatoni or penne. // **SERVES 4**

⅓ cup dried porcini mushrooms
¾ cup water
1 tablespoon olive oil
1 small onion, diced (about 1 cup)
2 large cloves garlic, chopped
2 tablespoons chopped fresh basil
½ cup red wine

½ teaspoon salt
¼ teaspoon freshly ground pepper
½ teaspoon red pepper flakes
3 cups fresh or 1 (28-ounce) can crushed tomatoes
    or tomato sauce
3 cups rigatoni or other tube-shaped pasta, cooked al dente
9 ounces skinless, boneless chicken breast, sliced into strips

Place the dried mushrooms in a bowl, cover them with the water, and let them soak for 15 minutes. Remove the mushrooms, reserving the soaking liquid. Chop the mushrooms.

Heat the olive oil in a large sauté pan over low-medium heat. Add the onions and cook for 5 minutes. Add the garlic and sauté for 2 to 3 more minutes.

Add the basil, wine, salt, pepper, and chili flakes. Simmer for 5 minutes. Add the tomatoes and mushrooms along with the mushroom soaking liquid. Stir to combine. Simmer gently over medium heat for 30 minutes.

While the sauce simmers, cook the pasta.

Ladle 1½ cups of sauce into a large skillet. Lay the raw chicken over the sauce. Place a lid on the skillet and simmer over medium heat for 5 minutes. Toss with the hot cooked pasta and the rest of the sauce.

Soba Noodles with Vegetables

Soba noodles are a traditional Japanese buckwheat noodle. They have an earthy flavor and a soft texture and are high in protein. We like soba noodles that are 60 percent buckwheat and 40 percent wheat. Toasted sesame oil and a high-quality soy sauce are essential for finishing this dish. // **SERVES 4**

1 (8.8-ounce) package soba noodles

2 tablespoons vegetable oil

1 medium onion, sliced

1 pound firm tofu, cut into 1-inch cubes

3 tablespoons soy sauce

1 to 2 carrots, sliced

1 cup cauliflower florets or chopped cabbage

1 to 2 cups broccoli florets (or another green vegetable)

2 tablespoons minced fresh ginger

1½ tablespoons maple syrup or mirin (optional, but delicious)

Red pepper flakes (optional)

Toasted sesame seed oil

Soba Noodles with Vegetables

Soba noodles cook quickly, so make sure to prepare all the vegetables before you start cooking. If you start cooking the noodles and the vegetables at the same time, they will be ready to serve at the same time.

Cook the noodles in boiling water as directed on package.

Heat the oil in a large sauté pan or wok over high heat. Add the onion, tofu, and 2 tablespoons of the soy sauce and cook, covered, for 2 minutes.

Stir in the carrots, cauliflower, broccoli, ginger, maple syrup, and red pepper flakes (if using), and about 3/4 cup water. Continue cooking, covered, for about 5 minutes or just until the vegetables are done but not soft. You want the broccoli to be bright green and firm. Do not overcook.

Add the last tablespoon of soy sauce to the pan or at the table.

Serve the vegetables and tofu over the soba noodles and drizzle with toasted sesame oil.

Black Bean Chili

At Spoonriver, this is a lunchtime favorite. We sprinkle it with grated cheese and roasted pumpkin seeds and serve it with either warm tortillas and salsa or our buttermilk cornbread (page 216). This chili also makes a great filling for enchiladas! // **SERVES 6 TO 8**

2 tablespoons olive oil or vegetable oil
1 large onion, chopped
4 cloves garlic, minced
2 large carrots, diced
2 stalks celery, chopped
1 red bell pepper, seeded and chopped
2 or 3 jalapeños, seeded and minced
2 (15-ounce) cans black beans, drained

1½ teaspoons dried oregano
1 tablespoon chili powder
2 teaspoons cumin
½ teaspoon cayenne
1½ teaspoons salt
Juice of half a lime
1 ounce unsweetened chocolate
2 tablespoons soy sauce

Heat the oil in a large pot and sauté the onion until it is soft. Add the garlic, carrots, and celery and sauté for another 5 minutes. Add the red bell pepper and chopped jalapeños. Sauté for 3 to 5 minutes longer.

Add the beans to the sautéed vegetables along with the oregano, chili powder, cumin, cayenne, salt, lime juice, chocolate, and soy sauce. Simmer over low heat for at least 15 to 20 minutes.

Lentil Vegetable Loaf

We love this with mashed potatoes and a favorite tomato sauce. With a green vegetable, it is vegetarian comfort food. **|| SERVES 6 TO 7**

⅓ cup barley
1 cup lentils
1 carrot, finely grated (½ cup)
½ cup diced onion
1 stalk celery, diced (½ cup)
1 parsnip, grated (½ cup)
1 tablespoon olive oil

2 tablespoons tamari or soy sauce
½ cup tomato sauce
1 egg
½ cup bread crumbs
1 tablespoon fresh herbs, chopped, or 1 teaspoon dried herbs
½ teaspoon salt
Freshly ground pepper

Rinse the barley in cold water and drain it well. Pick through the lentils, looking for any bad lentils or rocks. Clean the lentils by rinsing them several times with cold water. Combine the lentils and barley in a saucepan with 2½ cups of water. Bring the water to a boil and then turn the heat down to low and cook slowly until all of the water is absorbed, approximately 45 minutes to 1 hour.

Preheat the oven to 350 degrees and oil a loaf pan.

Sauté the carrots, onion, celery, and parsnip in the olive oil until the vegetables are soft, approximately 5 minutes. Combine the sautéed vegetables with the barley and lentils. Stir in the tamari and tomato sauce. Add the egg, bread crumbs, herbs, and salt and stir well. Season with pepper to taste.

Turn the mixture into the prepared loaf pan. Cover the pan with aluminum foil.

Bake for 55 minutes, uncovering the pan for the last 10 minutes. Remove the pan from the oven and place it on a rack to cool. Let the loaf sit for 10 to 15 minutes before serving.

Buttermilk Crepes with Ricotta and Vegetables

This recipe doesn't need a sauce. We prefer to dice a few tomatoes and sprinkle them with balsamic vinegar and a pinch of salt for a light and colorful topping. This filling is versatile: try different vegetables like spinach, chard, asparagus, or broccoli. Olives or walnuts make a nice addition. Two crepes and a salad are a complete meal, or serve one crepe with a grain (try wild rice or quinoa) and a salad. // SERVES 4 WITH 2 CREPES PER SERVING

CREPE BATTER//
¾ cup buttermilk
¾ cup milk
3 eggs
½ tablespoon honey
5 tablespoons butter, melted
¼ teaspoon salt
¼ cup whole wheat pastry flour or unbleached
    all-purpose flour
1 cup unbleached all-purpose flour

Whisk together the buttermilk, milk, eggs, and honey. Add the melted butter and salt, stirring to combine. Whisk in the flour.

Let the crepe batter rest a few hours in the fridge before using it. You can make the batter a day ahead.

Lightly oil a 9- to 10-inch nonstick pan. Heat the pan over medium heat until it is hot but not scorching. You may need to reheat the pan between crepes to maintain an even heat.

Ladle ¼ cup, or a little less, of batter into the pan, swirling it to get an even light coating. When the crepe is lightly browned, flip it with a long flexible spatula. Flip each crepe once, cooking it only a few minutes on each side.

FILLING//
1 tablespoon olive oil
1 cup finely diced carrots or red bell peppers
2 cups diced leeks (white and green parts)
8 ounces mushrooms, sliced
15 ounces ricotta cheese
Zest of half a lemon
2 teaspoons chopped fresh thyme
⅛ teaspoon grated nutmeg
½ teaspoon salt
¼ teaspoon pepper

To keep the crepes from sticking to each other, stack them on two plates, alternating the stack you add to, so a crepe hot off the pan isn't on a still-warm crepe.

Preheat the oven to 350 degrees.

To make the filling, heat the olive oil in a 12-inch skillet and sauté the carrots, leeks, and mushrooms over high heat, stirring several times, until the carrots are tender, approximately 7 minutes.

Combine the sautéed vegetables, ricotta cheese, lemon zest, thyme, nutmeg, salt, and pepper in a bowl. Stir well to combine.

This is enough filling for 8 crepes. You can roll the filled crepes or fold them in quarters after placing filling on one quarter of the crepe. Place the filled crepes on a cookie sheet or in a ceramic baking dish. Bake for about 15 minutes, covered loosely.

SPOONRIVER CREPE STAND //

Spoonriver has wanted to share in the community of the market as a participant ever since the Mill City Farmers Market started in 2006, but we were always too busy with other market business and running the restaurant. In 2010, we opened our Crepes by Spoonriver stand, serving several varieties of sweet and savory crepes. People really love the stand, and we have a tremendous amount of fun being out there with our market community, while simultaneously serving a very busy brunch at Spoonriver. We are able to absorb the energy from the market, take a break after brunch, and get ready for our busy Saturday dinner rush. Preparing and selling great crepes at the market is better than any cooking demonstration and a delicious way to spotlight Spoonriver's mission.

Brenda and the crepe crew at the Mill City Farmers Market

Commonplace Veggie Burger

This is my oldest recipe, updated a few times over the past thirty-five years. Yikes! I started making this recipe at Commonplace Restaurant in St. Paul when I was fifteen. If you have a food processor, please get it out; it makes quick work of mincing the vegetables, beans, and nuts. To mince the vegetables, simply chop them first into one-inch pieces and then pulse them. // **MAKES 12 TO 14 BURGERS**

¾ cup peanuts or pumpkin seeds
¾ cup sesame seeds
¾ cup sunflower seeds
1 (15-ounce) can chickpeas
2 tablespoons olive oil
1 medium onion, minced
5 cloves garlic, minced
1 stalk celery, minced
1 large carrot, minced or grated
1 teaspoon dried thyme or 2 teaspoons fresh

3 cups cooked brown rice (1 cup rice cooked in 2 cups water)
1 teaspoon dried oregano
¼ cup chopped fresh parsley
1 teaspoon chili powder
2 teaspoons paprika
1 teaspoon salt
Pepper
1 egg
¼ cup tamari or soy sauce
¼ cup bread crumbs, if needed

Roast the peanuts, sesame seeds, and sunflower seeds. If you buy them already roasted, look for nuts and seeds that are not salted. If you are roasting them, preheat the oven to 350 degrees. Place the nuts and seeds on a dry cookie sheet and roast them for 10 to 15 minutes, until they are fragrant but not browned. Cool the nuts and seeds before coarsely chopping them in a food processor.

Coarsely chop the chickpeas in a food processor or by hand.

Heat olive oil in a large skillet. Sauté the onions until they are soft. Add garlic and cook briefly before adding celery and carrots. Cook, stirring, until vegetables are soft, about 5 minutes.

Combine nuts, seeds, vegetables, cooked rice, chickpeas, thyme, oregano, parsley, chili powder, paprika, salt, and pepper in a large bowl. Stir to combine well. Beat the egg and tamari together and mix into the burger mixture until well incorporated. If the mixture is quite wet, add the bread crumbs. The mixture needs to be slightly sticky to form patties.

Using your hands, form a handful (about ½ cup) of the mixture into a patty that is about 3 inches in diameter and ¾ to 1 inch thick. Press the mixture together well.

To cook the veggie burgers, heat some vegetable oil in a heavy-bottomed skillet over medium-high heat. You need only enough oil to cover the bottom of the pan. Fry the patties until they are golden brown on each side and heated through. Make sure your flame is not on high, or they will brown too quickly.

To store any uncooked patties, wrap them well in plastic wrap or waxed paper and put them in the refrigerator or freezer. They will keep for 5 days refrigerated. The patties can be crumbly after freezing. Thaw them slowly and firmly press them together again before cooking.

Commonplace Veggie Burger

Lamb Spoonburger

This is a Moroccan spiced burger lightened by the addition of quinoa. These are delicious served as little cocktail meatballs with a Mediterranean spiced tomato or yogurt mint sauce. **// MAKES 7 PATTIES OR 40 (1-INCH) BALLS**

½ cup quinoa or bulgur
1 pound ground lamb
2½ tablespoons currants
1 tablespoon chopped garlic
½ teaspoon ground coriander
¼ teaspoon paprika
½ teaspoon cinnamon
1 teaspoon ground cumin
1½ teaspoons fennel seeds

¼ teaspoon cayenne
1 heaping tablespoon chopped fresh mint or 1 teaspoon dried
1½ teaspoons salt
1 teaspoon ground pepper
1 small egg
½ tablespoon tomato paste or ketchup
1 teaspoon fresh lemon juice
1 tablespoon olive oil

Bring 1 cup of water to a boil. Add the quinoa. Reduce the heat, cover the pan, and simmer for 10 minutes. Turn off the heat and let the grain steam, covered, for 5 minutes.

Combine all of the ingredients and mix them well, mashing until all the herbs are well incorporated. Form the mixture into patties or small balls.

Patties can be grilled, broiled, or sautéed. Appetizer-size lamb balls may be baked at 400 degrees, alone or in a sauce, for 10 to 12 minutes.

Lamb or Chicken Kebabs in a Mediterranean Marinade

Either lamb or chicken work really well with this simple marinade. If you don't have a grill, you can also prepare these under a broiler. These kebabs go very well with the Couscous Platter with Grilled Vegetables (page 121). If you are using wooden skewers, be sure to soak them in water for 20 minutes. // **SERVES 3**

¼ cup olive oil
2 tablespoons lemon juice
Grated zest of 1 lemon
1 teaspoon paprika
4 cloves garlic, minced
3 tablespoons chopped fresh cilantro, parsley, mint,
    or a combination
½ teaspoon salt
Pepper
12 ounces boneless chicken breast or lamb, cut into
    1- to 1½-ounce pieces

In a bowl, whisk together the olive oil, lemon juice, zest, paprika, garlic, herbs, salt, and pepper. Pour the marinade over the meat and allow it to marinate for 1 to 2 hours, stirring occasionally to coat the meat evenly.

Skewer the meat and prepare the grill. Grill the kebabs over medium heat, turning a few times until cooked through. Chicken should be thoroughly cooked; lamb can be pink at the center.

Lamb and Chicken Kebabs in a Mediterranean Marinade

Chicken Stew

ENTRÉES

You could make this stew with chicken breasts instead of thighs. Simply cut them into large pieces and treat them the same way as the thighs. You can season the flour with a combination of dried herbs or with just salt and pepper. || **SERVES 6**

8 boneless, skinless chicken thighs
½ cup unbleached all-purpose flour seasoned with
    ½ teaspoon salt and ½ teaspoon pepper
2 tablespoons vegetable oil
1 cup diced onion
1 tablespoon chopped garlic
1 bay leaf

½ teaspoon dried sage
2 cups chicken stock
3 to 4 carrots, chopped into 1-inch pieces (2 cups)
3 medium Yukon gold or russet potatoes, quartered (3 cups)
1 stalk celery, sliced
½ cup peas
Salt and pepper

Cut the thighs in half if they are large. Rinse them in cold water, but don't dry them. Thoroughly coat the damp chicken pieces in the seasoned flour.

Heat the oil in a 4- to 5-quart heavy-bottomed Dutch oven or soup pot. Brown the chicken on both sides, about 10 minutes. It works best to do this in batches. Transfer the browned chicken to a platter. Put the onions in the pot. Cook for a few minutes, stirring, until the onions soften. Add the garlic, bay leaf, sage, and stock. Bring to a simmer and cook 15 minutes, covered.

Add the carrots, potatoes, and celery, and cook for another 15 minutes. Return the chicken to the pot and cook for another 10 minutes, or until the carrots and potatoes are tender. Place the peas on top of the stew, cover the pot, and steam the peas for 3 to 4 minutes. Stir in the peas and season the stew with salt and pepper to taste.

BRAUCHER'S SUNSHINE HARVEST FARM //

Mike and Colleen Braucher own Braucher's Sunshine Harvest Farm near Webster, Minnesota. Theirs is a small family farm, committed to sustainable farming practices, that raises grass-fed beef and lamb, pasture-raised pork, and chickens and eggs. They do not feed antibiotics or use hormones and other chemicals on any of their animals.

Studies show that grass-fed beef is higher in omega-3 fatty acids, CLA (conjugated linoleic acid, a beneficial fat), and vitamins A and E than conventional grain-fed beef. Omega-3s are formed in the green leaves (specifically, the chloroplasts) of plants. Sixty percent of the fat content of grass is a type of omega-3 fatty acid called alpha-linolenic acid, abbreviated ALA or LNA. Omega-3s are most abundant in seafood and certain nuts and seeds such as flaxseeds and wal-nuts, but they are also found in grass-fed animal products. Omega-3 fatty acids play a vital role in every cell and system in your body. Of all the fats, they are the most heart friendly. Because grass-fed meat is so lean, it is also lower in calories. For example, a sirloin steak from a grass-fed steer has about one-third to one-half the amount of fat as a similar cut from a grain-fed steer.

Spoonriver gets all of its beef, which has been dry aged for fourteen days, from the Brauchers. In fact, Colleen likes how we prepare her beef so much that she will often stay for a steak when she makes her delivery to the restaurant.

Mike Braucher and friends

Sauces for Grilled Steak or Chicken

At Spoonriver, we are able to serve wonderful grass-fed beef supplied by Braucher's Sunshine Harvest Farm in Webster. They dry age it for fourteen days and we marinate it in olive oil and herbs and grill it medium rare. We always serve our steaks with a potato or grain and an abundant amount of vegetables and top them with any one of these sauces.

Bleu Cheese–Walnut Butter Sauce

This sauce is also great on beets, asparagus, hamburgers, and bread. // **MAKES ½ CUP**

1½ tablespoons walnuts
½ cup unsalted butter, softened
3 ounces bleu cheese, crumbled
1 green onion, sliced
¼ teaspoon salt
Pinch of freshly ground pepper

In a small, dry skillet, toast the walnuts over medium-high heat for 3 to 5 minutes, tossing frequently. Let cool.

Chop the walnuts. Combine the walnuts, butter, bleu cheese, green onions, salt, and pepper in a bowl. Mix well.

Roasted Red Bell Pepper Butter // **MAKES 1 CUP**

1 red bell pepper
½ cup unsalted butter, softened
1½ tablespoons minced shallot
1 large garlic clove, minced
1 teaspoon finely chopped fresh thyme
1 teaspoon paprika
½ teaspoon salt
⅛ teaspoon freshly ground pepper

There are several ways to roast a pepper. If you have a gas range, turn the burner on high and place the pepper directly on the grate. Using tongs, turn the pepper to char all sides evenly. You can also do this over a grill. To roast a pepper in the oven, place the pepper under the broiler, turning until the pepper is charred all over.

As soon as the pepper is blackened, place it in a bowl and cover it with a lid or plastic wrap to let the pepper steam. Let cool. Gently remove all of the charred skin. Cut the pepper in half and remove the seeds. Chop the pepper into small pieces.

Combine the roasted pepper, butter, shallots, garlic, thyme, paprika, salt, and pepper in a bowl and mix well. Serve at room temperature.

Honey Rosemary Butter // **MAKES ½ CUP**

3 tablespoons fresh rosemary leaves
½ cup unsalted butter, softened
1 tablespoon honey
2 teaspoons freshly ground pepper
¼ teaspoon salt

Finely chop the rosemary. Combine it with the butter, honey, pepper, and salt and mix well.

Serve at room temperature.

Rib eye steak with Chimichurri Sauce

Horseradish Sour Cream // MAKES 1½ CUPS

4 tablespoons prepared horseradish
8 ounces sour cream
2 tablespoons chopped green onions or chives
2 tablespoons fresh chopped parsley
2 teaspoons lemon juice or white wine
¼ teaspoon salt
¼ teaspoon freshly ground pepper

Combine all of the ingredients in a bowl and stir well.

Chimichurri Sauce // MAKES 1 CUP

½ cup olive oil
2 tablespoons red wine vinegar
2 tablespoons lime juice
1 small onion, diced fine
⅓ cup chopped fresh cilantro
4 cloves garlic, minced
1 tablespoon chopped fresh oregano
¼ teaspoon cayenne
¼ teaspoon freshly ground pepper
¼ teaspoon salt

Combine all of the ingredients in a bowl and mix well.
Cover and chill for 2 to 3 hours before serving.

Herbed Pork Tenderloin with Applesauce

Fischer Farms supplies our pasture-raised pork. It's so important to support local small farms that raise pork in a humane and sustainable way. Marinating meat in herbs is a healthy, old-world method of cooking meat that may prevent the harmful carcinogens produced by grilling. // **SERVES 4**

PORK TENDERLOIN //
2 tablespoons finely chopped fresh rosemary
2 tablespoons finely chopped fresh sage
2 tablespoons finely chopped fresh thyme
1½ tablespoons finely chopped fresh parsley
4 (5-ounce) portions pork tenderloin
Vegetable oil
Salt and pepper

APPLESAUCE //
4 apples, peeled, cored, and quartered
½ cup apple juice or water
1 small cinnamon stick
Juice of half a lemon
½ teaspoon salt

Combine all of the herbs. Toss the tenderloins in a little vegetable oil to coat. Sprinkle them with salt and pepper. Roll the tenderloins in the herbs to coat.

Preheat the oven to 350 degrees.

Select an ovenproof skillet that will fit all of the meat with some space between. Put enough vegetable oil in the skillet to coat the bottom of the pan. Sear the meat on both sides. Place the pan in the oven and bake until the temperature is 150 degrees in the center or until the center is slightly pink, about 6 to 8 minutes. If you do not have a skillet that is large enough or that can go in the oven, sear the meat on the stove and then place the meat on a sheet pan to go in the oven. Let the pork rest for a few minutes before serving.

To make the applesauce, combine the apples, apple juice, cinnamon stick, lemon juice, and salt in a small saucepan. Bring the juice to a simmer over medium heat and cook, covered, until the apples are soft. Cool. Remove the cinnamon stick and puree the apples in a blender or food processor.

White Fish with Persian Nut Crust and Yogurt Mint Sauce

This flavorful and nutritious crust works well with any white fish. Serve the fish with a yogurt sauce or drizzle it with pomegranate molasses. We recommend a pilaf and greens or a citrus salad to accompany the fish. // **SERVES 4**

YOGURT MINT SAUCE //
½ cup plain low-fat yogurt
1 tablespoon lemon juice
½ cup chopped cilantro or mint
Pinch of salt

FISH //
½ cup sesame seeds
1 cup pistachios, chopped fine in a food processor
2 teaspoons dried oregano
2 teaspoons ground coriander
⅛ teaspoon ground allspice
Salt and pepper
1 pound (4 good-sized fillets) fish
Egg wash (1 egg beaten with 1 tablespoon water)
Vegetable oil for sautéing

Combine the yogurt, lemon juice, cilantro, and salt. Taste the sauce. You may want to add a little more lemon or salt. Refrigerate the sauce until it is needed.

Combine the sesame seeds, pistachios, oregano, coriander, allspice, salt, and pepper in a shallow dish that will hold a whole fish fillet.

Dredge a fish fillet through the egg wash. Place the fillet on top of the crust mixture and lightly press the fish down to adhere the crust to the egg coating. Turn the fish over to coat both sides. Repeat with the remaining fillets.

Heat the vegetable oil in a sauté pan large enough to fit the fillets without crowding. You may need to cook them in batches or use more than one pan. When the oil is hot, add the fish and cook until golden brown on one side; then turn and cook the other side.

Serve the fish with a dollop of the sauce on each fillet. Put the rest in a small dish to add at the table as desired.

FISH AND SEAFOOD //

Fresh fish and seafood has always been our biggest seller at Spoonriver. Our recipes suggest specific fish to use, but these are only guidelines. There are numerous other kinds of fish you can use with each recipe. Take advantage of what is in season: using what is fresh is always the best option. I have been fortunate to have Coastal Seafoods as our reliable and knowledgeable seafood vendor for 30 years! We might be in the Midwest, but we get wonderful fresh seafood, thanks to the relationships they have built with fishermen.

There are four basic cooking methods for preparing fish: sautéing, poaching, broiling, and grilling. It is not difficult or unlike cooking other foods. The worst thing you can do to fish is overcook it. Timing is the most important factor in preparing a meal with fish. Most often, the fish should be the last item prepared, so try to ready the rest of the meal ahead of time and devote your attention to the fish.

Sautéing or Panfrying

For sautéing, use a good vegetable oil, butter, or olive oil. Butter tastes great but burns at a low temperatu e. We use clarified butter at Spoonriver. It's easy to make and allows you to cook at a higher ten rature without fear of burning. You can also use half oil and half butter.

How much oil to use depends on the type of pan you are using. A nonstick skillet will require only one tablespoon of oil. If using a cast-iron or copper pan, you will need about two tablespoons. When the fish is breaded or in a nut crust, you will need more oil or butter because the crust absorbs the fat: you will need about four tablespoons of oil or enough to coat the pan with about 1/8 inch of oil.

The thinner the fish fillet, the higher the heat can be. With a thick fillet or a whole fish, a lower temperature allows the middle to cook before the outside gets overdone. Sautéed fish fillets take approximately 8 to 10 minutes per inch of thickness to cook through.

Poaching

The advantage of poaching is that it requires no fats, is quick and easy, and doesn't interfere with the taste of delicately flavored fish. Fish is poached by simmering it gently in just enough liquid to cover. The poaching liquid can be as simple as lightly salted water with a few lemon slices and herb sprigs.

Bring the liquid to a simmer in a skillet large enough to hold the fish with liquid to cover. Gently slide the fish into the simmering liquid. If there is not enough liquid to cover the fish, add a little hot water.

Poach for 8 minutes per inch of thickness of fish. If you are unsure whether the fish is done, cut into a piece with a small paring knife. The flesh should separate easily and have changed color. When it is time to take the fish out of the pan, slide a long, wide spatula under the fish lengthwise and carefully lift it out.

Broiling and Grilling

Broiling is essentially upside-down grilling. Line a broiler pan or a sheet pan with foil to catch the drips, to keep the fish from sticking, and to ease cleanup. Oil the fish or the foil to avoid sticking. When grilling, oil the fish well so it does not stick to the grill.

The best distance from the flame depends on the thickness of the fish. A half-inch-thick fillet should be broiled about 2 to 3 inches from the heat. A fillet or a whole fish that is 1 to 2 inches thick should be 4 to 6 inches from the flame.

When putting a glaze on the fish during the last minute or two of cooking, place the fish about 6 inches from the broiler so the glaze will heat through and form a nice crust without burning.

Cook the fish for about 8 minutes per inch of thickness. Check by cutting into the thickest section and checking for opaque flesh that separates easily.

Sautéed Walleye in a
Poppy Seed–Cornmeal Crust

This is a simple way to serve any flaky white fish fillet. // **SERVES 4**

¼ cup cornmeal
¼ cup poppy seeds
Grated zest of 1 lemon
½ teaspoon kosher salt
Freshly ground pepper
1 egg

¼ cup milk
1¼ pounds white fish fillets (choose whatever is freshest),
    skin removed
Vegetable oil, for sautéing
Lemon wedges, for serving

Combine the cornmeal, poppy seeds, lemon zest, salt, and pepper in a shallow bowl or platter. In another shallow bowl, whisk together the egg and milk with a fork to create an egg wash.

Rinse the fillets and pat them dry. Dip the fish in the egg wash and then roll it in the cornmeal mixture to coat both sides.

Sauté the fish in a hot skillet coated with a little vegetable oil, cooking it approximately 4 minutes on each side. Cooking time will depend on the thickness of the fillets.

Serve with fresh lemon wedges.

Walleye or Bass with Sesame Crust and Ginger Orange Teriyaki

This preparation is great with any flakey white fish. Try it with walleye, cod, or striped bass. Serve it with a simple white or brown rice and vegetables. Black sesame seeds are a beautiful addition to the crust but are not necessary. Play with the sauce recipe: use passion fruit, mango, blackberry, or raspberry puree or pomegranate molasses in place of the orange juice concentrate. Leftover sauce is delicious on vegetables, chicken, steak—you name it. // SERVES 4 WITH SAUCE LEFT OVER

GINGER ORANGE TERIYAKI SAUCE //

⅔ cup soy sauce
¼ cup mirin
⅓ cup maple syrup or brown sugar
1 tablespoon finely grated or minced fresh ginger
2 tablespoons frozen orange juice concentrate

Place the soy sauce, mirin, maple syrup, and ginger in a medium saucepan. Bring the mixture to a boil; then turn down the heat to low and simmer the sauce for about 20 minutes. Be careful that the sauce does not boil over or burn. You want a nice syrupy texture. Don't let the sauce get too thick, though, or it will become salty and concentrated.

Remove from the heat and cool slightly before adding the orange juice concentrate. Stir to combine. Serve the sauce at room temperature. Leftover sauce will keep for 4 to 6 weeks in the refrigerator.

FISH //

½ cup sesame seeds
2 tablespoons black sesame seeds (optional)
¼ cup cornmeal or unbleached all-purpose flour
¼ teaspoon salt
5 tablespoons vegetable oil
1¼ pounds skinless fish fillets

To prepare the fish, remove the skin and bones, if necessary. If the fish is in one piece, cut it into four portions. When sautéing fish with a crust, it is important that the fillets are not thicker than ¾ inch. If the fish is too thick, the crust will burn before the fish is fully cooked.

Mix the white and black sesame seeds (if using), cornmeal, and salt. Dredge the fish in the sesame mixture to coat.

Heat the oil in a large skillet. Add the fish and sauté it over medium heat until it is golden brown on each side, about 3 to 4 minutes per side (see page 153).

Serve with about a tablespoon of the sauce drizzled over each piece of fish.

Walleye with Sesame Crust and Ginger Orange Teriyaki

Broiled Char with Orange Miso Glaze

This glaze is a perfect match for oily fish such as salmon, mackerel, or char. Its tangy ginger-citrus combination tempers the richness of the fish. You can prepare the glaze well ahead of time. It will keep in the refrigerator for up to two weeks. Only rice and some seasonal vegetable are needed to complete a meal. **// SERVES 4**

2 inches ginger root, peeled
2 tablespoons frozen orange juice concentrate
2 tablespoons mirin

Grate the peeled ginger; then squeeze the ginger tightly in your hand to extract the juice. You should have about 1 tablespoon of ginger juice. Mix together the ginger juice, orange juice concentrate, mirin, and miso, and stir until smooth.

3 tablespoons white or light miso
.1½ pounds fish fillets
Toasted sesame oil

Clean and dry the fish fillets and lightly rub the bottom sides with toasted sesame oil. Place the fish in a baking dish.

Broil the fish for 5 minutes about 3 to 4 inches from the flame. Then spoon a generous amount of glaze on each fillet and continue broiling until the fish is opaque, about 5 more minutes. Watch carefully. You can brown the glaze, but do not allow it to burn.

Salmon with Wasabi Glaze and Asian Pesto

In this dish, the richness of the salmon is balanced by the zing of wasabi. Wasabi adds a little heat and a fuller flavor, but you can leave it out if you prefer. Adding coconut milk to the pesto contributes a fragrant tropical note to this dish. This is lovely served with a very simple jasmine rice. // **SERVES 4**

ASIAN PESTO //

ves garlic

blespoon chopped fresh ginger

cups (½ bunch) lightly packed cilantro leaves

s cup lightly packed basil leaves

¼ cup sliced or slivered almonds

1 teaspoon toasted sesame oil

1 cup coconut milk

¾ cup unsweetened shredded coconut

1 teaspoon salt

3 tablespoons lime juice

To make the pesto, mince the garlic and ginger in a food processor. Add the cilantro, basil, almonds, sesame oil, coconut milk, coconut, salt, and lime juice and pulse. Do not overdo it; some texture is good. Set the pesto aside.

Now make the glaze. Whisk together the garlic, ginger, mus... abi, honey, rice vinegar, soy sauce, and vegetable oil in a small bowl. If the ginger is stringy, squeeze out the juice with your hand and use the ginger juice instead of the ginger.

WASABI-GLAZED SALMON //

1 clove garlic, minced

1-inch piece of ginger, grated

2 tablespoons yellow mustard powder

1½ tablespoons wasabi powder

2 tablespoons honey

1 tablespoon rice vinegar

½ tablespoon soy sauce

1 tablespoon vegetable oil

4 (5- to 6-ounce) salmon fillets

Broil the salmon 6 inches away from the flame. Brush on the glaze 2 to 3 minutes before the salmon is done. Cooking time will vary depending on the thickness of the fish, but 8 minutes per inch of thickness is typical. If the fish is too close to the flame, you may burn the glaze. Watch it closely: you only need 2 to 3 minutes for the glaze to heat and form a shiny crust on the fish.

Serve the salmon with the pesto on the side.

Snapper with Cranberry Ginger Sauce

This sauce is good all year long. Ginger adds a spicy touch to the fruit glaze. New potatoes or a potato-parsnip puree and steamed snow peas go well with this dish. **// SERVES 4 WITH SAUCE LEFT OVER**

CRANBERRY GINGER SAUCE //
2-inch piece of ginger, peeled
1 cup cranberries
1 ⅓ cups black cherry or other fruit juice
1 tablespoon grated orange rind (preferably organic)
3 tablespoons mirin (or sake or white wine sweetened with honey)

Grate the peeled ginger root. Then squeeze the grated ginger tightly in your hand to extract the juice. You will need 1 tablespoon.

Combine the cranberries, juice, orange rind, and mirin in a saucepan. Bring the mixture to a boil. Boil hard for 5 minutes to reduce the juice.

Remove the pan from the heat and add the ginger juice. Cool the sauce slightly and puree it in a blender until very smooth. Taste the sauce. We like it a little tangy; others may prefer to add a touch of honey. (Leftover sauce will hold in the refrigerator for two weeks. Try it on turkey, chicken, or buckwheat croquettes.)

SNAPPER //
4 (5- to 6-ounce) fresh snapper fillets
Flour for dredging fillets
2 to 3 tablespoons vegetable oil

Dredge the snapper fillets in flour. Heat the vegetable oil in a skillet. Sauté the fish fillets in the hot oil for about 4 minutes on each side, depending on their thickness. The fish should be golden brown.

Serve the fish with warm cranberry ginger sauce.

COASTAL SEAFOODS //

Spoonriver, and Cafe Brenda before it, relies on Coastal Seafoods in Minneapolis to supply us with an incredible selection of fresh seafood from all over the world. Coastal Seafoods opened our midwestern eyes to how amazing fresh seafood could be. What Coastal Seafoods brought to the Twin Cities thirty years ago was really significant. Before that, we had to buy frozen fish from a restaurant broker.

Coastal Seafoods deals directly with small boats and suppliers, and it shows in the quality and variety available to us at Spoonriver. Some of our favorites, which you will find on our menu, are Icelandic haddock, Canadian walleye, Lake Superior herring, Alaskan rockfish, and Caledonian shrimp.

The first call Brenda makes every morning is to Coastal to see what is available that day. The daily delivery is a big event in the kitchen. The continuity of this twenty-five-year business relationship is invaluable, and the consistency of their product is absolutely amazing.

Suzanne Weinstein, owner of Coastal Seafoods

Broiled Fresh Rainbow Trout
with Pomegranate–Brown Butter Sauce

This is a unique fusion of browned butter and pomegranate molasses that can't be denied. If you haven't procured a bottle of this Lebanese pomegranate molasses yet, it is time for a field trip to a food market that carries imported ingredients. Simple jasmine rice and some sexy Mediterranean vegetables would be lovely with this. This sauce is also great on broiled fresh sole. **// SERVES 6**

3 tablespoons butter
2 tablespoons vegetable oil
1 tablespoon minced shallot
½ tablespoon minced ginger
½ teaspoon dried mustard
1 tablespoon pomegranate molasses or 3 tablespoons
    lime juice with a little zest

Salt and pepper
1 teaspoon honey
Pinch of cayenne (optional)
6 small rainbow trout, boned
Vegetable oil, for broiling

Slowly brown the butter in a saucepan set over low heat, being careful not to burn it. After the butter stops sizzling and foaming, it will begin to brown. Watch closely and remove the pan from the heat when the butter is amber brown and smells toasty, nutty, and sweet.

Pour the butter out of the pan so it stops cooking and add the oil to it. Let the butter cool slightly, but not so long that it hardens.

Put the shallots, ginger, mustard, pomegranate molasses, salt, pepper, honey, and cayenne (if using) in a blender. Blend on medium and then slowly add the butter mixture while blending until all is creamy. The sauce will thicken, or emulsify, and change color.

Serve this sauce at room temperature on broiled rainbow trout or a white fish of your choice.

To broil the trout, set the broiler to medium. Brush sides of the fish with oil and season with salt and pepper. Place the fish on a sheet pan and broil for a few minutes. The fish should flake easily when tested with a fork.

Poached Trout with Berry Vinaigrette

This is a very fresh, light sauce for trout or other white fish. We like to serve it with blanched asparagus or green beans and either boiled new potatoes or a simple rice pilaf with pecans. It is an extremely pretty and colorful plate and may be served hot or cold. You can broil or bake the fish if you would like to skip the poaching. // **SERVES 4 WITH EXTRA SAUCE**

ERRY VINAIGRETTE //

2 cups apple-blackberry juice

1 cup blackberries or raspberries (fresh or frozen),
     plus extra for garnish

Juice of 1 lemon

½ cup vegetable oil

White pepper

Salt

POACHED TROUT //

4 cups water

1 onion, sliced

1 carrot, sliced

1 stalk celery, sliced

1 stem fresh parsley

3 to 4 whole star anise

3 bay leaves

Salt

A few peppercorns

1 cup dry white wine or 1 tablespoon lemon juice

4 (8- to 10-ounce) trout

Pour the juice into a saucepan, place it over medium-high heat, and simmer until the juice is reduced to ½ cup.

W   berries well. Puree 1 cup of the berries and the re   in a blender, and strain the puree through a fine-   to remove the seeds from the puree.

Combine the b   y puree and lemon juice in a bowl. Whisk in the oil and then the salt and pepper, mixing until combined. Set the sauce aside.

Prepare the poaching stock by combining the water, onion, carrot, celery, parsley, star anise, bay leaves, salt, peppercorns, and wine in a saucepan. Simmer the stock for 20 minutes, and then strain it.

Pour the strained stock into a shallow pan over medium heat. Bring the stock to a boil, reduce it to a low simmer, and place the fish in the pan. Cover the pan. Gently simmer the fish for approximately 6 to 8 minutes, depending on the thickness of the fish. Remove the fish from the pan as soon as they are done and drain them on a paper towel. Place the fish on plates and top them with the vinaigrette, with additional berries as a garnish.

Mahi-Mahi with Mango Salsa

Mango salsa is a refreshing addition to sautéed or grilled fish. Any white-fleshed fish is well accented by this tropical salsa. Try it with mahi-mahi, snapper, or rock fish. In the winter, when we need to be transported out of Minnesota, this helps if we can't get on a plane. Ripe mangoes should give slightly when you press on them with your thumb. **// SERVES 6**

MANGO SALSA//
1½ cups peeled, seeded, and chopped ripe mango
2 to 3 tablespoons lime juice
Pinch of nutmeg
¼ teaspoon ground coriander
¼ teaspoon ground cardamom
2-inch piece ginger root, peeled
1 tablespoon chopped fresh mint
1 jalapeño, minced
Pinch of salt
Cayenne or chili paste (optional)

SAUTÉED MAHI-MAHI//
2 to 2½ pounds mahi-mahi fillets
Vegetable oil or clarified butter
Flour for dredging fish

Measure out ¾ cup of the chopped mango and set it aside. Puree the remaining ¾ cup mango with the lime juice until it is very smooth.

In a bowl, mix together the pureed and chopped mango. Add the nutmeg, coriander, and cardamom.

Finely grate the ginger root. Squeeze the ginger tightly in your hand to extract ½ tablespoon of ginger juice. Discard the pulp.

Add the ginger juice, mint, and jalapeño to the mango mixture. Mix well. Season lightly with salt and add cayenne or chili paste (if using). You can serve the salsa either at room temperature or chilled.

Heat about ⅛ inch of oil in a skillet over medium-high heat. Dredge the fish fillets in the flour and sauté them, turning once, until the flesh is opaque and the fish is lightly browned. Cooking time will vary depending on the thickness of the fish.

Top the fish with a dollop of salsa before serving.

Mahi-Mahi with Mango Salsa

Caribbean Fish and Shrimp Stew

This is a wonderful fish stew with a rich and unique flavor. Make this stew with either shrimp or fish. If you are lucky enough to get some fresh conch, try it! It really is delicious. A loaf of bread or some flour tortillas with the stew makes a satisfying meal. // **SERVES 4**

FISH STOCK //

2 tablespoons butter or vegetable oil

1 onion, chopped, or the green tops of a leek, sliced

4 cloves garlic, minced

Fish scraps or shrimp heads and peels

1 carrot, sliced

1 stalk celery, sliced

5 cups water

STEW //

1 tablespoon butter or vegetable oil

1 large onion, chopped

5 cloves garlic, minced

4 carrots, sliced

2 large potatoes, peeled and cut into 1-inch cubes

1 jalapeño, minced (optional)

2 ripe plantains or 1 yam, sliced thin

1 (14-ounce) can coconut milk

4 cups fish stock, homemade or from soup base

1 pound shrimp

1 pound firm white fish

Juice of 1 lime

Salt

Freshly ground pepper

Sprigs of fresh coriander, for garnish

First make the fish stock. Melt the butter in a soup pot. Sauté the onion, garlic, and fish scraps for 3 to 5 minutes. Add the carrot and celery, and continue to sauté for another 5 minutes. Add the water. Bring it to a boil, and then reduce the heat and gently simmer for 30 minutes. Strain the stock, reserving the liquid.

When you are ready to make the stew, melt the butter in a large soup pot. Sauté the onions and garlic until the onions are translucent, about 3 to 5 minutes. Add the carrots, potato, and jalapeño, and sauté for 5 minutes. If you are using yam instead of plantain, add it now.

Add the coconut milk and fish stock, and bring it to a boil. Reduce the heat to a simmer, and cook until the carrots and potato are quite tender, approximately 5 minutes. If you are using plantains, add them to the stew now and simmer for 10 another minutes.

Add the fish and shrimp and cook until flaky and tender. Add the lime juice, salt, and pepper to taste.

Garnish each bowl with fresh cilantro.

Salmon Served on Lentil Stew
with Horseradish Sour Cream

This is nice served with new potatoes and greens. **// SERVES 4**

2 cups French lentils
1 tablespoon olive oil
1 medium onion, diced
2 carrots, sliced
1 stalk celery, diced
1 fennel bulb, diced (about 1 cup)
1 tablespoon minced garlic
4 cups water or vegetable stock
1 (15-ounce) can tomato puree or crushed tomatoes
    (1¾ cups)
1 bay leaf
1 tablespoon chopped fresh thyme or 1½ teaspoons dried
½ teaspoon salt
Freshly ground pepper
20 ounces salmon fillet, divided into 4 (5-ounce) portions

HORSERADISH SOUR CREAM //
½ cup sour cream
1 tablespoon freshly grated or jarred horseradish
1 teaspoon lemon juice
Pinch of salt

Sort through the lentils, picking out any small rocks or debris, and then rinse them.

Heat the olive oil in a saucepan. Sauté the onions over medium heat until they are soft, about 3 minutes. Add the carrots, celery, fennel, and garlic. Cook for 5 more minutes. Add the water, tomatoes, bay leaf, thyme, lentils, salt, and pepper. Bring the water to a boil; then turn it down to a simmer and cook over medium-low heat for 30 to 35 minutes, until the lentils are tender.

Meanwhile, prepare the horseradish sour cream. Combine the sour cream, horseradish, lemon juice, and a pinch of salt in a bowl. Stir well and taste. Add more horseradish as needed, depending on how strong you want it and the potency of the horseradish.

Poach or broil the salmon until the center of the fish is just cooked through. The fish will feel slightly firm and have a light pink color in the center.

Serve the fish fillets on top of the lentil stew with a dollop of the horseradish sour cream on top.

Black Cod or Salmon in Asian Broth

This is our favorite comfort food in the cold months. Salmon and rich white fish work well, or make this dish with tofu for a delicious vegetarian option. You can make the stock in advance; it keeps up to a week in the refrigerator. **// SERVES 4 GENEROUSLY**

STOCK//

1 medium onion, quartered

2 carrots, unpeeled, washed and cut into 1-inch pieces

1 stalk celery, sliced

¼ cup sliced fresh ginger

4 cloves garlic, smashed

1 teaspoon salt

6 whole peppercorns

2 whole star anise

1 bay leaf

¼ teaspoon red pepper flakes

1 (2-inch) square kombu (optional)

9 cups water

½ cup soy sauce

2 tablespoons mirin

2 teaspoons rice vinegar

2 tablespoons maple syrup or honey

¼ to ½ teaspoon chili paste

FISH//

1 small onion, sliced

1 carrot, sliced, or 1 cup thinly sliced winter squash

1 red bell pepper, cut into large squares

1 cup napa cabbage or bok choy

1 cup peapods

16 to 20 ounces black cod or salmon, skinned and cut into 4 portions, or tofu, cut into 1-inch cubes

Rice, Chinese, or wheat noodles

To make the stock, combine the onion, carrots, celery, ginger, garlic, salt, peppercorns, star anise, bay leaf, red pepper flakes, kombu (if using), and water in a pot. Bring the water to a boil, reduce it to a simmer, and simmer, covered, for 30 to 40 minutes. Strain the stock, pressing the liquid from the vegetables. Discard the vegetables. Add the soy sauce, mirin, rice vinegar, maple syrup, and chili paste.

To prepare the broth, place all of the stock and the onion, carrot, red bell pepper, and cabbage in a saucepan and cook for about 5 minutes. If you are preparing tofu rather than fish, add the tofu to the broth when you add the vegetables. Add the peapods and cook for 2 more minutes.

Meanwhile, broil the fish. The cooking time will vary depending on the thickness of the pieces and the type of fish. Although you could try poaching the fish in the broth, it works best to broil the fish separately and top each bowl of broth with a piece of fish.

Cook the noodles according to the package directions, timing them to be done at the same time as the fish and vegetables. Strain the noodles, but do not rinse them.

Serve this dish in low wide bowls. Place the noodles in the bottom of the bowls, ladle the vegetables and broth over them, and top each with a piece of broiled fish.

Salmon in Asian Broth

Salmon Potato Cakes

Salmon cakes are a delicious way to serve canned fish. This recipe can easily be made with leftover mashed potatoes. Serve the salmon cakes with a green salad, coleslaw, or braised vegetables.

// SERVES 4

15 ounces canned wild salmon

2 cups cooked and gently mashed potatoes

1 bunch green onions, sliced into thin rounds

1 egg, beaten

1 teaspoon salt

Freshly ground pepper

Bread crumbs or cracker crumbs

Vegetable oil

Pinch of smoked paprika or chipotle powder (optional)

Remove the skin from the salmon. Leave the bones, they have lots of calcium and are very soft. Put the salmon in a mixing bowl.

Add the mashed potatoes, green onions, egg, salt, and pepper. Mix together well. Form the mixture into 8 patties, dredge them in bread crumbs, and set them on a plate.

Braised vegetables are a great accompaniment to Salmon Potato Cakes.

Heat a large skillet and add 3 tablespoons of oil. When the oil is hot, place the patties in the pan with some space between them. You may have to cook them in batches or use two pans. Cook over medium heat for 3 to 5 minutes per side until they are golden brown.

Sautéed Walleye with Pickled Cucumber Tartar Sauce

Pickled cucumber tartar sauce is great served with grilled or sautéed fish. It can be prepared in advance and kept in the fridge for a week or so. It is great on a fish sandwich. **// SERVES 4 TO 6**

⅓ cup diced pickles
1 tablespoon chopped fresh dill
2 tablespoons chopped green onion
1 garlic clove, minced (optional)
1 teaspoon Dijon mustard
Lemon or lime juice

½ cup good mayonnaise, either homemade or a jarred
    natural mayo
Pepper
1½ pounds walleye fillets (ask the fishmonger to skin
    and bone the fish)

Place the pickles, dill, green onions, garlic (if using), mustard, lemon juice, and mayonnaise in a bowl and stir to combine.

To prepare the fish, see the instructions on page 153.

CROQUETTES

CROQUETTES are very versatile. Made of grains and vegetables, they can easily be a light lunch or a hearty dinner entrée. They can be served plain or with a sauce. The combinations are endless: ours are combinations of grains, vegetables, spices, and nuts mixed together and formed into patties. Fried in a little oil, they become crisp cakes.

Once you have tried some of our suggestions and mastered the consistency and cooking methods, you will have discovered a new use for grains and a great way to use up leftover potatoes and grains.

Croquettes should be somewhat tricky to hold together while cooking. Here are some suggestions for getting the mixture to hold together. Add an egg if your mixture seems dry and does not hold together when you press it in your hand (we have listed an optional egg in many of the recipes). Another method to try, with or without an added egg, is to put half of the croquette mixture in a food processor or grinder. Process for 30 to 60 seconds; then add it back to the remaining mixture and stir well to combine. This step develops the gluten in the grains, helping to bind the ingredients together. Do not process too much; you want some texture left in the croquette mixture.

To avoid problems while forming the croquettes, start with clean hands and rinse your hands often. If your hands are slightly wet, the mixture won't stick to them as much. When forming croquettes, it is important to be firm and really compress them. If they are not pressed together well, they will fall apart while cooking.

When cooking croquettes, use a hot skillet with enough oil to coat the bottom of the pan. You do not need a lot of oil. Do not crowd the patties in the pan; be sure to leave space between them. Cook each side of the patties until they are golden brown, and turn them only once. They tend to break apart with any extra handling. If you have leftover croquette mixture, form it into patties before refrigerating. Patties will keep for several days when they are well wrapped.

Brown Rice, Almond, and Vegetable Croquettes

This is a great way to use leftover rice, but there is a trick to getting it to stick together. Leftover rice is often dry, and we have found that it helps to steam it. If it is still not sticky enough, grind some of it up and mix it back into the remaining rice. Try replacing the almonds with another nut variety: they all work well and each adds its distinct flavor. Serve these croquettes with squash and a mixed green and vegetable salad.

// MAKES 16 CROQUETTES (8 SERVINGS)

ROASTED ONION–MISO SAUCE//

6 medium onions

1 head garlic

3 tablespoons brown miso

Salt

½ to 1 cup water or vegetable stock

CROQUETTES//

1½ cups short-grain brown rice

3½ cups water

1 teaspoon salt

¾ cup slivered almonds

1 tablespoon vegetable oil

½ cup minced celery

¾ cup grated sweet potato, carrot, or parsnip

¾ cup minced green onion

⅓ cup chopped fresh parsley

1 tablespoon soy sauce

Vegetable oil for sautéing

Heirloom garlic offers a wide array of flavors, from mild to sharp, sweet to spicy.

Preheat the oven to 425 degrees. Place the whole onions and the head of garlic on a baking sheet. Bake for 45 minutes and remove the garlic. Continue to bake the onions approximately 15 more minutes, or until they soften. If you are using small onions, 45 minutes will probably be enough for them too. Remove the pan from the oven and let the onions cool enough that you can peel them.

When the garlic is cool enough to handle, cut the bottom off the garlic bulb and squeeze out the roasted garlic. Put the peeled onions, garlic, miso, and salt in a blender and puree. Add as much water or stock as necessary to reach the desired consistency.

While the vegetables are roasting, prepare the rice for the croquettes. Combine the rice, water, and salt in a saucepan, and bring the water to a boil. Cover the pan and turn down the heat to a low simmer. Cook for approximately 45 minutes, or until all the water has been absorbed. Set the rice aside to cool slightly.

Reduce the oven temperature to 350 degrees. Roast the almonds for 15 minutes. Let them cool a bit and then coarsely chop them.

In a large skillet, heat the vegetable oil over medium heat. Add the celery and sweet potatoes, and sauté for a few minutes. Add the green onions and sauté for one more minute.

In a large bowl, mix together the sautéed vegetables, parsley, soy sauce, almonds, and rice.

Form the mixture into 3-inch patties. Sauté the patties in vegetable oil in a large skillet until they are golden brown on both sides.

Serve the croquettes with warm Roasted Onion–Miso Sauce.

Buckwheat Potato Croquettes with Ginger Mushroom Sauce

Ideal for fall and winter, these hearty croquettes will keep you warm and strong. Serve them with steamed cauliflower, broccoli, or greens. Dry roasting the groats makes their flavor nutty and delicious.
// **MAKES 14 CROQUETTES (7 SERVINGS)**

SAUCE //

½ ounce ounce dried shiitake mushrooms
4 cups water (including the water used for soaking mushrooms)
1 large onion, sliced
1 medium carrot, sliced
5 cloves garlic, smashed
1 tablespoon star anise
¼ cup chopped ginger root
½ teaspoon salt
1 tablespoon toasted sesame oil
1½ cups sliced button mushrooms
1 to 2 tablespoons tamari or soy sauce
2½ tablespoons cornstarch or arrowroot
¼ cup water for dissolving cornstarch

CROQUETTES //

1½ cups buckwheat groats
3½ cups water
1 teaspoon salt
1 small onion, diced small
1 tablespoon olive oil or vegetable oil
2 medium potatoes, diced small (about 2 cups)
1 stalk celery, diced small
1 small carrot, diced small
¼ cup tahini
2 tablespoons chopped parsley
¼ cup finely chopped green onions
2½ tablespoons tamari or soy sauce
Vegetable oil for sautéing

Soak the shiitake mushrooms in water for 30 minutes. Reserve the water and slice the mushrooms.

Combine the water, onion, carrot, garlic, anise, ginger, and salt in a saucepan. Bring to a boil; then reduce heat to low. Simmer the stock, covered, for 20 minutes and then strain it.

Sauté the button and shiitake mushrooms in the sesame oil for 3 to 5 minutes; then add them to the strained stock. Add the tamari or soy sauce. Dissolve the cornstarch or arrowroot in a little bit of water, and then stir it into the sauce. Bring the sauce to a boil, stirring often, until it thickens.

Dry roast the buckwheat groats in a dry, heavy skillet set over medium-low heat, cooking and stirring for about 8 minutes. Let the groats cool a few minutes before adding the water and salt. Be careful: the pan is hot and will sizzle when you add the water. Cover and cook over low

heat until the water is gone and the groats are cooked, approximately 20 minutes, 25 if you skipped roasting them.

Sauté the onions in the olive oil until they are translucent. Add the potatoes and ½ cup of water and cook 5 minutes. Add the celery and carrot and cook for another 3 to 5 minutes, until the vegetables are soft. Add a few more tablespoons of water if necessary.

Combine the groats, sautéed vegetables, tahini, parsley, green onions, and tamari. Let the mixture cool to room temperature before forming it into 2-inch patties.

Put enough vegetable oil in a large frying pan (a cast-iron, nonstick, or heavy-bottomed skillet will work well) to coat it well. Heat the oil over medium-high heat. Sauté the patties until they are crispy and golden brown. Add more oil if needed to make the patties fry crisply. Turn the patties over only once.

Jasmine Rice and Black Bean Croquettes

Demand for croquettes has earned them a place on our weekend menu. Prepared with endless combinations of grains, nuts, vegetables, and spices, they are influenced by many different cultures. We serve them topped with a sauce that suits the style and the vegetable side dishes. We would top these croquettes with a fresh mango or tomato salsa. Remember to sauté them until they are crispy on both sides.

// MAKES 16 CROQUETTES (8 SERVINGS)

2 cups jasmine rice, rinsed
2¾ cups water
1 teaspoon salt
1 tablespoon olive oil
3 to 4 carrots, grated (1½ cups)
1 bunch green onions, minced

1 (15-ounce) can black beans, drained and rinsed
¼ teaspoon ground cumin
½ teaspoon ground coriander
Pepper
3 to 4 tablespoons vegetable oil for sautéing

Combine the rice, water, and salt in a saucepan. Bring the rice to a boil; then cover the pan, reduce the heat, and simmer for 12 minutes. Turn off the heat and let the rice sit, still covered, for 5 minutes. When the rice has cooled slightly, stir it firmly for a few minutes so the rice gets sticky.

Heat the olive oil in a skillet and sauté the carrots for 3 minutes. Add the green onions, a pinch of salt, and 1 tablespoon of water. Cook for 1 minute.

Combine the rice, beans, sautéed vegetables, cumin, coriander, and pepper in a large bowl, and mix well with a wooden spoon.

Form the mixture into 2- to 3-inch patties, firmly shaping and pressing them together so they stay together.

Sauté the croquettes in hot vegetable oil until they are golden brown and crispy on both sides. A nonstick pan works well. Cook all of the patties and freeze those you don't eat, or reheat them the next day.

Jasmine Rice and Black Bean Croquettes

Brown Rice and Nori Croquettes

Serve the rice patties with the nori on top so the nori doesn't get soggy. We like to just tear the nori in pieces and wrap it around bites of rice. It's a great way to get nutritious and delicious nori into our diets. We serve extra toasted nori on the side. || **MAKES 6 PATTIES (6 SERVINGS)**

1½ cups short-grain brown rice
3¾ cups water (use 3¼ cups if using long-grain rice)
½ teaspoon sea salt

Nori sheets (one sheet per patty)
6 tablespoons vegetable oil
Soy sauce, for garnish

In a saucepan, combine the rice, water, and salt. Bring it to a boil; then turn the heat down to low, cover the pan tightly, and cook for 45 to 50 minutes. The cooking time needed can vary 5 minutes or so either way, depending on the size of your pan and how high the heat is: just make sure the water is all evaporated.

Stir the rice firmly with a large wooden spoon or fork to make it a little sticky. Let the rice cool slightly so you can shape it into patties. Wash your hands, but don't dry them completely: damp hands will help you as you firmly shape the rice into 6 patties.

Fold each nori sheet two times to make about a 4-inch square. Set the nori aside.

Heat 4 tablespoons of the oil in a skillet over medium (not low) heat. Sauté the croquettes until they are crispy and golden brown, approximately 5 minutes per side. Add the other 2 tablespoons of oil when you turn the patties so the grains of rice get nice and crunchy.

When the patties are completely cooked, place one folded sheet of nori under each patty and cook the nori almost a minute over medium heat. It is nice to char the nori a touch, but be careful not to burn it.

You can easily store uncooked patties in the fridge for a few days and cook them when you want to eat them.

Tempeh Potato Croquettes with Peanut Sambal

This Indonesia—inspired entrée is very nice served with a fresh, light cucumber-mint salad and lightly braised spinach, onions, and tomatoes. Try adding some coconut milk and lime to the braised vegetables.

// MAKES 10 CROQUETTES (5 SERVINGS)

PEANUT SAMBAL //
2 fresh hot green chilies, stemmed and seeded
4 cloves garlic
1 cup roasted peanuts
1 tablespoon soy sauce
2 tablespoons fresh lime juice
3 tablespoons raisins
1 tablespoon honey

CROQUETTES //
6 small to medium potatoes (2 cups mashed)
1 (8-ounce) cake tempeh, cut into 4 pieces
5 tablespoons vegetable oil
1½ tablespoons minced garlic
1 teaspoon dried coriander
1 teaspoon dried cumin
2 carrots, grated (1 cup)
1 bunch green onions, minced (1 cup)
2 teaspoons salt
Freshly ground pepper
1 egg, beaten
2 tablespoons chopped parsley

Put the green chilies, garlic, peanuts, soy sauce, lime juice, raisins, and honey in a food processor and grind into a chunky paste. Do not overprocess; the sambal is better with some texture. Set the sambal aside for now.

Peel and boil the potatoes until they are easily pierced with a fork, approximately 20 minutes. Drain the potatoes, mash them with a little of the boiling water or some milk, and set them aside.

Heat 2 tablespoons of the vegetable oil. Sauté the tempeh over medium heat for approximately 3 minutes or until it is golden brown.

Turn the tempeh, and add the garlic, coriander, and cumin. Break up the tempeh pieces with a fork as you stir in the spices. This will keep the spices from burning and help the tempeh absorb them.

Turn down the heat to low and cook for 2 to 3 minutes. Transfer the tempeh to a bowl and set it aside. When it is cool, crumble up the tempeh.

Heat 1 tablespoon of the oil. Sauté the carrots and green onions for 1 to 2 minutes.

Combine the mashed potatoes with the tempeh and sautéed vegetables. Add the salt, pepper, egg, and parsley. Stir well.

Form the mixture into 3-inch patties. Sauté them in 2 tablespoons of hot vegetable oil until they are golden brown on both sides. Serve with peanut sambal on the side.

Chickpea Vegetable Croquettes with Tahini Lemon Sauce

These croquettes are similar to falafel balls. They are very flavorful and rich when topped with tahini lemon sauce. We enjoy them with pita bread and steamed vegetables, such as green beans and cauliflower, or a salad. If you want to go all out for a special dinner, grilled eggplant is nice too. Olives are a must! // **MAKES 8 CROQUETTES (4 SERVINGS)**

TAHINI LEMON SAUCE //
1 cup tahini, stirred well
½ cup water
Juice of 2 lemons
3 cloves garlic, finely chopped
2 tablespoons chopped fresh parsley
½ teaspoon salt

CROQUETTES //
2 (15-ounce) cans chickpeas
1½ tablespoons olive oil
1 small onion, finely chopped
1 carrot, grated
3 cloves garlic, crushed
1 stalk celery, finely diced
½ teaspoon turmeric
1½ teaspoons ground coriander
1 teaspoon paprika
¼ teaspoon cayenne
1½ teaspoons salt
1 egg, beaten
Vegetable oil for sautéing
½ cucumber, peeled, seeded, and diced (optional)
1 cup diced tomato (optional)

Combine the tahini, water, lemon juice, garlic, parsley, and salt in a bowl and whisk until very smooth. Depending on how thick the tahini is, you may need to adjust the amount of water to get the right consistency. Chill the sauce until you need it.

Drain and mash the chickpeas. A food processor works well, or you can mash them by hand.

Heat the olive oil over medium heat. Sauté the onions, carrots, garlic, and celery for 3 to 5 minutes.

Combine the mashed chickpeas and the sautéed vegetables with the turmeric, coriander, paprika, cayenne, salt, and egg. Stir well. If the mixture is too wet, add up to ½ cup of bread crumbs.

Form croquettes that are about 2 inches in diameter. Cook them in hot vegetable oil until they are well browned on both sides. Serve the croquettes with tahini lemon sauce. Garnish them with diced cucumber and tomatoes, if desired.

Mediterranean Roasted Eggplant Croquettes with Tomato Basil Sauce

Roasted eggplant has a rich, smoky flavor that blends well with fresh mint. Serve the croquettes on a bed of pasta that you have tossed with olive oil, parsley, salt, and pepper. Add a green vegetable or a simple green salad to complete the meal. // **MAKES 12 CROQUETTES (6 SERVINGS)**

CROQUETTES//
2 to 3 medium eggplants
4 tablespoons olive oil
1 cup finely diced onion
½ cup finely grated Parmesan cheese
½ cup bread crumbs
1 large egg
1 tablespoon chopped fresh mint or 1 teaspoon dried
1 tablespoon chopped parsley
Salt and pepper
Flour

TOMATO BASIL SAUCE//
12 large roma tomatoes or 1 (28-ounce) can
    roasted tomatoes
2 tablespoons olive oil
6 cloves garlic, minced
2 tablespoons chopped fresh basil
Salt and pepper

Roast the whole eggplant directly over the flames on the stove, turning until it is charred evenly on all sides, approximately 5 minutes. The center of the eggplant should be soft. If you are using large eggplants, you can finish cooking them in the oven: place whole eggplants in a 400-degree oven until they are soft in the center. The eggplant will feel soft and can be pierced easily with a fork. Let the eggplant cool until you can touch it. Peel the eggplant and finely chop the flesh.

Sauté the onion in 1 tablespoon of olive oil for 3 to 5 minutes.

Combine the roasted eggplant and sautéed onion with the Parmesan, bread crumbs, egg, mint, parsley, salt, and pepper. Chill the mixture for approximately 45 minutes. The mixture will not be really firm, but it should hold together when sautéed. If it is too loose, add some more bread crumbs.

Make the sauce while the croquette mixture chills. Place the washed tomatoes under the broiler. Watch them carefully: when one side is lightly browned, turn the tomatoes over and roast the other side until they are lightly browned. This takes about 10 minutes. Remove the tomatoes from the broiler and let them cool. Peel, seed, and finely chop or process the tomatoes. If you are using canned roasted tomatoes, skip this step.

Sauté the garlic in the olive oil. Add the chopped tomatoes, fresh basil, salt, and pepper. Simmer for 5 minutes.

Gently shape the chilled croquette mixture into 2-inch patties, and carefully dip them in flour. Sauté the patties in the remaining 3 tablespoons of olive oil until they are golden brown. Serve the croquettes with warm tomato basil sauce.

Tofu Walnut Croquettes

Tofu walnut croquettes are perfect served with brown rice, soy sauce, and a side vegetable. These are also good as tofu meatballs served with spaghetti. We like to toast the walnuts to bring out the flavor of the nuts, but it is not necessary. If you choose to toast the nuts, place them on a sheet pan in a 350-degree oven for 8 to 10 minutes until they are fragrant and lightly browned. // **MAKES 8 CROQUETTES (4 SERVINGS)**

1 large carrot, grated
1 stalk celery, minced
1 teaspoon dried herbs (thyme, basil, marjoram, parsley, or a combination)
2 tablespoons vegetable oil
4 green onions, cut in half lengthwise and thinly sliced
1 package firm tofu

½ cup toasted walnuts, chopped small
⅓ cup bread crumbs
2 medium eggs or 1 large egg, beaten
1½ tablespoons soy sauce
Salt and pepper

Sauté the carrot, celery, and herbs in a skillet with ½ tablespoon of the oil for a few minutes. Add the green onions and sauté for another minute.

Crumble the tofu in a bowl. Add the walnuts, bread crumbs, eggs, sautéed vegetables, soy sauce, and salt, and pepper. Using a fork, mash and stir the mixture until the ingredients are evenly blended. Form the mixture into 2- to 3-inch patties.

Heat the remaining 1½ tablespoons of oil in a skillet. Sauté the croquettes until they are golden brown on both sides.

breads

BREADS //

MAKING BREAD can be very satisfying. Each loaf starts with the basics—flour, water, and yeast—but I continually experiment, adding cracked grains, seeds, different flours, or dried fruits. Each loaf is different but always nourishing and delicious.

Yeast is a living organism, reacting to temperature and moisture. Our hurried, hectic lives create a desire for instant gratification. When I first started baking bread, I used a lot of yeast and put my dough in the warmest spot in the house. My dough rose quickly, and I had large loaves in a few hours. I didn't realize that my bread had little texture or flavor until I started sampling bread from small artisan bakeries. As I learned to use less yeast and let the dough rise slowly at room temperature, I discovered that the bread had a more complex grain flavor and a chewier, denser texture.

The first section in this chapter features loaves made with a poolish. *Poolish* is a French word for a premix of fermenting dough. A poolish can be started two to eight hours before you start your bread.

The second section is direct-rise breads. Most of us learned to bake bread this way. I still encourage a slow rise. These loaves require about five hours from start to finish.

The third section is quick breads: sweet breakfast or tea loaves, scones, and muffins.

The Washburn A Mill used to grind enough flour to make 12 million loaves of bread per day. Today, it is the site of the Mill City Museum and the Mill City Farmers Market.

POOLISH is a starter dough that is allowed to sit and ferment for a few hours or overnight. The poolish should be used the same day or within 24 hours. The mixture will rise and fall if the dough sits a long period. Using a poolish allows you to use a smaller amount of yeast than the direct-rise method. A smaller amount of yeast and a longer rising time result in a loaf with a nice crumb and a chewy texture.

Flour

Wheat is essential for a good loaf of bread. It is the only grain that contains the two proteins that make up gluten, the super protein. Gluten provides structure for yeast dough. When the dough is kneaded, the gluten develops, forming weblike strands in the dough that stretch and expand, trapping carbon dioxide as the dough rises during fermentation. Bread flour has the optimum percentage of protein, but unbleached all-purpose flour also has high levels of protein. Whole wheat flour contains the bran

portion of the wheat kernel. The bran is coarse and cuts through the gluten strands during fermentation, creating a very dense loaf. A good flour mixture for bread is 1 cup of whole wheat flour for every 3 cups of unbleached all-purpose flour or bread flour. You can mix the flours together in a large bowl before you start making the bread, or you can mix the flour when you buy it and store the flour mixture in an airtight container. Whole wheat flour will become rancid at room temperature far quicker than white flour will, so it is best to store whole wheat flour in the refrigerator.

Other flours and grains may contain some protein but not enough to form the gluten necessary for bread making. Adding a small quantity of oats, corn, rye, sesame, and other grains and seeds adds variety and nutrition to our breads. Experiment with additions, substituting other flours and grains for 1 to 1½ cups of the flour mix.

Whole Wheat Country Loaf

This is a basic wheat loaf with a nice crust. The bread recipes that follow in this section are variations on this recipe. // **MAKES 2 LOAVES**

POOLISH //

½ teaspoon active dry yeast
¾ cup warm water (about 75 degrees)
1 cup unbleached all-purpose or bread flour

DOUGH //

5 to 6 cups unbleached all-purpose or bread flour
2 cups whole wheat flour
2 cups warm water
½ teaspoon active dry yeast
1 tablespoon salt

Prepare the Poolish

Combine the yeast and water in a large bowl. Let it sit a few minutes for the yeast to dissolve. Stir in the flour. The mixture will be wet, resembling pancake batter. Stir vigorously for a few minutes. Cover the bowl with plastic wrap to keep the poolish from drying out. Place the bowl in a warm, draft-free place for 2 hours to overnight. The longer the poolish sits, the more sour and yeasty it becomes.

Make the Dough

Combine the flours in a bowl.

When the poolish is ready, it will be full of little bubbles and have a very yeasty aroma. Add the water to the poolish and stir to combine. Add the yeast and stir again. Add the salt and 1 cup of the flour. As you stir, add more flour 1 cup at a time until you have a thick, shaggy dough. The dough is ready to knead when it is still a little sticky but not wet.

Turn the dough onto a floured table. Knead, adding more flour as needed to keep the dough from sticking. Knead for at least 10 minutes to develop the gluten. The dough will become soft and pliable. It is ready when the dough holds

its shape when you form it into a ball and springs back lightly when you push your finger into it.

Place the dough in a large oiled bowl. Turn the dough to coat it all over with oil. Cover the bowl with plastic wrap or a towel. Place it in a warm, draft-free place to rise until it has doubled in size, about 2 hours. The dough has risen enough when a finger pressed ½ inch into the dough leaves an indentation.

Turn the dough out of the bowl onto a floured surface. Turn the dough several times, kneading it to deflate the dough. Divide the dough in half.

Shape the Loaves

Traditionally, bread is risen in baskets and baked directly on a baking stone in the oven. This results in a loaf with a very nice crust. If you have baskets made for bread rising, flour them and place the dough directly in the baskets. If you are using other baskets, line the basket with a linen napkin or towel that you have dusted with flour. Shape the dough into an oval or round shape to match the shape of your basket. Place the dough in the basket seam-side up. Cover the dough and let it rise for 1½ to 2 hours.

Turn the bread gently onto a peel or board dusted with cornmeal. Make several cuts into the top of the loaf with a very sharp or serrated knife. Carefully slide the bread from the peel onto the baking stone.

You can also use loaf pans instead of baskets. Butter the pans and let the dough rise in the pans. Make several slices in the top of the loaves before baking them.

Preheat the oven to 425 degrees about 45 minutes to an hour before you want to bake. If you are using a baking stone, place it in the oven when you turn it on so it is heated through before you start baking.

Bake the loaves for 30 minutes, checking them after 20 minutes. Turn the loaves if they are baking unevenly. Bread is done when it is golden brown and sounds hollow when you thump the bottom with your fingers. If the loaf still sounds dense, place it back in the oven and check again in 5 minutes.

Variations

You can substitute other flours or grains for up to 1½ cups of the flour. Rolled oats, oat bran, rye, wheat germ, and cracked wheat are all good options. You can also add seeds and dried fruit. Try oats and sesame seeds or pumpkin seeds and dried cranberries.

You can also add a sweetener such as sugar, honey, or molasses if you want a sweeter breakfast loaf. Use ½ to 1 cup for a two-loaf batch. A loaf with sugar will have a darker crust, so don't assume it is done because it has browned early. Bake each loaf for the full 30 minutes.

Sesame Oat Bread

Sesame seeds are high in protein. When raw, they add a nice crunch to bread. If you gently toast them in a dry skillet until they are lightly browned, they will also add a deliciously nutty flavor. Oats create a moist texture while adding fiber. // **MAKES 2 LOAVES**

POOLISH//
½ cup warm water (about 75 degrees)
½ teaspoon active dry yeast
¾ cup unbleached all-purpose or bread flour

DOUGH//
2 cups warm water (about 75 degrees)
½ teaspoon active dry yeast
1 cup rolled oats (not quick oats)
1 tablespoon salt
½ cup sesame seeds
3 to 3½ cups unbleached all-purpose or bread flour
1½ cups whole wheat flour
1 egg white

Prepare the Poolish

Combine the yeast and water in a large bowl. Let it sit a few minutes until the yeast dissolves. Add the flour and stir vigorously for a few minutes. Cover the bowl with plastic wrap and place it in a warm, draft-free place for 2 hours to overnight.

Make the Dough

Combine the flours in a bowl.

Place the warm water in a large bowl. Add the yeast and let it sit for a few minutes to dissolve the yeast. Add the rolled oats and let them sit for 30 minutes to soften the oats. This step is not absolutely necessary, but it improves the texture of the bread.

Add the poolish and stir to combine. Add the salt, sesame seeds, and 1 cup of the flour. Stir well. Continue adding flour 1 cup at a time until you have a stiff dough that forms a rough ball.

Turn the dough onto a floured surface and knead it, adding more flour as needed, until the dough is not sticky, about 10 minutes. Knead the dough, rhythmically pushing, turning, and folding it. The dough should be soft and elastic, springing back lightly when pinched.

Oil a bowl and place the dough in the bowl, turning the dough to coat it evenly with oil. Cover the bowl with plastic wrap or a towel. Let the dough rise until it has doubled in size, about 2 hours.

Punch down the dough and divide it in half.

Shape the Loaves

Traditionally, bread is risen in baskets and baked directly on a baking stone in the oven. This results in a loaf with a

Sesame Oat Bread

very nice crust. If you have baskets made for bread rising, flour them and place the dough directly in the baskets. If you are using other baskets, line the basket with a linen napkin or towel that you have dusted with flour. Shape the dough into an oval or round shape, depending on the shape of your basket. Place the dough in the basket seam-side up. Cover the dough and let it rise for 1½ to 2 hours.

Preheat the oven to 425 degrees for 30 to 45 minutes before you put the loaves in.

Brush the tops of the loaves with a beaten egg white and sprinkle them with oats and sesame seeds for a beautiful crust.

Gently move the loaves onto a peel or a board dusted with cornmeal. Make several cuts into the top of the loaf with a very sharp or serrated knife. Carefully slide the bread from the peel onto the baking stone.

Bake for 20 minutes; then turn the loaves and bake them for another 10 minutes. Tap the bottom of the loaf to see if it is done. If the crust is hard and the loaf sounds hollow when you tap the bottom, it is done. If the loaf sounds dense, return it to the oven and bake another 5 minutes.

Multigrain Bread

This is a hearty bread with a nice texture. The cracked wheat and rye give it a nutty flavor. You can add dried fruit, sunflower seeds, or both for a nice breakfast loaf. // **MAKES 2 LOAVES**

POOLISH//
½ teaspoon active dry yeast
¾ cup warm water (about 75 degrees)
1 cup unbleached all-purpose or bread flour

DOUGH//
2 cups warm water
½ teaspoon yeast
1 tablespoon salt
3 to 3½ cups unbleached all-purpose or bread flour
¼ cup cornmeal
¼ cup rye flour
⅓ cup ground flaxseed
⅓ cup cracked wheat
1 cup whole wheat flour

Prepare the Poolish

Combine the yeast and water in a large bowl. Let it sit a few minutes until the yeast dissolves. Add the flour and stir vigorously for a few minutes. Cover the bowl with plastic wrap and place it in a warm, draft-free place for 2 hours to overnight.

Make the Dough

When the poolish is ready, it will be full of little bubbles and have a very yeasty aroma. Add the water to the poolish and stir to combine. Add the yeast and stir again. Add the salt and 1 cup of the flour. As you stir, add the cornmeal, rye flour, flaxseed, cracked wheat, and whole wheat flour. Stir until all of the grains are well incorporated. Add more flour, 1 cup at a time, until you have a thick, shaggy dough. The dough is ready to knead when it is still a little sticky but not wet.

Turn the dough onto a floured table. Knead, adding more flour as needed to keep the dough from sticking. Knead for at least 10 minutes to develop the gluten. The dough will become soft and pliable. It is ready when the dough holds its shape when you form it into a ball and springs back lightly when you push your finger into it.

Place the dough in a large oiled bowl, turn the dough to coat it with oil, and cover the bowl with plastic wrap or a towel. Place the dough in a warm, draft-free place to rise for 2 hours.

Turn the dough out of the bowl onto a floured surface. Turn the dough several times, kneading it to deflate the dough. Divide the dough in two.

Shape the Loaves

Traditionally, bread is risen in baskets and baked directly on a baking stone in the oven. This results in a loaf with a very nice crust. If you have baskets made for bread rising, flour them and place the dough directly in the baskets.

If you are using other baskets, line the basket with a linen napkin or towel that you have dusted with flour. Shape the dough into an oval or round shape, depending on the shape of your basket. Place the dough in the basket seam-side up. Cover the dough and let it rise for 1½ to 2 hours.

Turn the bread gently onto a peel or board dusted with cornmeal. Make several cuts into the top of the loaf with a very sharp or serrated knife. Carefully slide the bread from the peel onto the baking stone.

You can also use loaf pans. Butter the pans and let the dough rise in the pans. Make several slices in the top of the loaves before baking them.

Preheat the oven to 425 degrees about 45 minutes to an hour before you want to bake. If you are using a baking stone, place it in the oven when you turn it on so that it is heated through before you start baking.

Bake the loaves for 30 minutes, checking them after 20 minutes. Turn the loaves if they are baking unevenly. Bread is done when it is golden brown and sounds hollow when you thump the bottom with your fingers. If the loaf still sounds dense, place it back in the oven and check again in 5 minutes.

Flaxseed, Dried Fruit, and Pumpkin Seed Bread

Flaxseed has high levels of omega-3 fatty acids and vitamin B and is full of fiber. You can grind it in a spice grinder and add it to every loaf you ever make, increasing the nutritional value of your bread. In this loaf, we use both whole and ground flaxseed. The whole seeds add texture and fiber to your loaf. We like to combine seeds with dried fruit for a sweet and colorful touch. This is a great morning bread when spread with butter or peanut butter. // **MAKES 2 LOAVES**

POOLISH//

½ teaspoon active dry yeast
¾ cup warm water (about 75 degrees)
1 cup unbleached all-purpose or bread flour

DOUGH//

2 cups warm water
½ teaspoon yeast
1 tablespoon salt
3 to 4 cups unbleached all-purpose or bread flour
1 cup whole wheat flour
¼ cup ground flaxseed
¼ cup whole flaxseed
½ cup dried cranberries
½ cup pumpkin seeds
½ cup cracked wheat (optional)

Prepare the Poolish

Combine the yeast and water in a large bowl. Let it sit a few minutes until the yeast dissolves. Add the flour and stir vigorously for a few minutes. Cover the bowl with plastic wrap and place it in a warm, draft-free place for 2 hours to overnight.

Make the Dough

When the poolish is ready, it will be full of little bubbles and have a very yeasty aroma. Add the water to the poolish and stir to combine. Add the yeast and stir again. Add the salt and 1 cup of the flour. Add the flaxseed, dried cranberries, and pumpkin seeds. As you stir, add flour 1 cup at a time until you have a thick, shaggy dough. The dough is ready to knead when it is still a little sticky but not wet.

Turn the dough onto a floured table. Knead, adding more flour as needed to keep the dough from sticking. Knead for at least 10 minutes to develop the gluten. The dough will become soft and pliable. It is ready when the dough holds its shape when you form it into a ball and springs back lightly when you push your finger into it.

Place the dough in a large oiled bowl, turn the dough to coat it with oil, and cover the bowl with plastic wrap or a towel. Place the dough in a warm, draft-free place to rise for 2 hours.

Turn the dough out of the bowl onto a floured surface. Turn the dough several times, kneading it to deflate the dough. Divide the dough in half.

Shape the Loaves

Traditionally, bread is risen in baskets and baked directly on a baking stone in the oven. This results in a loaf with a very nice crust. If you have baskets made for bread rising, flour them and place the dough directly in the baskets. If you are using other baskets, line the basket with a linen napkin or towel that you have dusted with flour. Shape the dough into an oval or round shape, depending on the shape of your basket. Place the dough in the basket seam-side up. Cover the dough and let it rise for 1½ to 2 hours.

Turn the bread gently onto a peel or board dusted with cornmeal. Make several cuts into the top of the loaf with a very sharp or serrated knife. Carefully slide the bread from the peel onto the baking stone.

You can also use loaf pans. Butter the pans and let the dough rise in the pans. Make several slices in the top of the loaves before baking them.

Preheat the oven to 425 degrees about 45 minutes to an hour before you want to bake. If you are using a baking stone, place it in the oven when you turn it on so that it is heated through before you start baking.

Bake for 30 minutes, checking the loaves after 20 minutes. Turn the loaves if they are baking unevenly. Bread is done when it is golden brown and sounds hollow when you thump the bottom with your fingers. If the loaf still sounds dense, place it back in the oven and check again in 5 minutes.

Variations

Try any of these combinations in place of the dried cran-berries and pumpkin seeds:

raisins and sunflower seeds
dried figs and hazelnuts
dried cherries and almonds

Hearty Wheat Bread

Wheat germ is the embryo of the wheat kernel. It is removed and separated from the grain when milling white flour. Wheat germ is rich in proteins, fats, minerals, and vitamins. Store wheat germ in the refrigerator because the oil in it quickly goes rancid at room temperature. Adding wheat germ and cracked wheat results in a nutritious loaf with a nice texture and a nutty flavor. // **MAKES 2 LOAVES**

POOLISH//
½ teaspoon active dry yeast
¾ cup warm water (about 75 degrees)
1 cup unbleached all-purpose or bread flour

DOUGH//
2 cups warm water
½ teaspoon yeast
1 tablespoon salt
⅓ cup wheat germ
½ cup cracked wheat
2 cups whole wheat flour
3 to 3½ cups unbleached all-purpose or bread flour

Prepare the Poolish

Combine the yeast and water in a large bowl. Let it sit a few minutes until the yeast dissolves. Add the flour and stir vigorously for a few minutes. Cover the bowl with plastic wrap and place it in a warm, draft-free place for 2 hours to overnight.

Make the Dough

When the poolish is ready, it will be full of little bubbles and have a very yeasty aroma. Add the warm water to the poolish and stir to combine. Add the yeast and stir again. Add the salt and 1 cup of the flour. Add the wheat germ and cracked wheat and stir well. Continue stirring and adding flour a cup at a time until you have a thick, shaggy dough. The dough is ready to knead when it is still a little sticky but not wet.

Turn the dough onto a floured table. Knead, adding more flour as needed to keep the dough from sticking. Knead for at least 10 minutes to develop the gluten. The dough will become soft and pliable. It is ready when the dough holds its shape when you form it into a ball and springs back lightly when you push your finger into it.

Place the dough in a large oiled bowl. Turn the dough to coat it with oil. Cover the bowl with plastic wrap or a towel. Place the dough in a warm, draft-free place to rise for 2 hours.

Turn the dough out of the bowl onto a floured surface. Turn the dough several times, kneading it to deflate the dough. Divide the dough in half.

Shape the Loaves

Traditionally, bread is risen in baskets and baked directly on a baking stone in the oven. This results in a loaf with a very nice crust. If you have baskets made for bread rising, flour them and place the dough directly in the baskets.

If you are using other baskets, line the basket with a linen napkin or towel that you have dusted with flour. Shape the dough into an oval or round shape, depending on the shape of your basket. Place the dough in the basket seam-side up. Cover the dough and let it rise for 1½ to 2 hours.

Turn the bread gently onto a peel or board dusted with cornmeal. Make several cuts into the top of the loaf with a very sharp or serrated knife. Carefully slide the bread from the peel onto the baking stone.

You can also use loaf pans. Butter the pans and let the dough rise in the pans. Make several slices in the tops of the loaves before baking them.

Preheat the oven to 425 degrees about 45 minutes to an hour before you want to bake. If you are using a baking stone, place it in the oven when you turn it on so that it is heated through before you start baking.

Bake the loaves for 30 minutes, checking them after 20 minutes. Turn the loaves if they are baking unevenly. Bread is done when it is golden brown and sounds hollow when you thump the bottom with your fingers. If the loaf still sounds dense, place it back in the oven and check again in 5 minutes.

direct-rise breads

DIRECT-RISE BREADS are made with yeast,
but all of the ingredients are mixed at one time.
Although direct-rise breads do not require a poolish,
or pre-ferment, you do have to allow time for rising.

Whole Wheat Bread

This is a basic recipe for loaves made without a starter. We like to use a small quantity of yeast and let the dough rise slowly at a moderate temperature. A little sugar or honey will help the yeast along and add to the flavor of the loaf, but you could leave it out. We like to use a mix of unbleached white bread flour and whole wheat flour. You can alter the quantities, using more whole wheat flour for a heartier loaf or more white flour for a softer loaf. // **MAKES 2 LOAVES**

2 teaspoons active dry yeast
2 cups warm water (about 75 degrees)
1 tablespoon salt

1 tablespoon sugar or honey
4½ cups unbleached bread or all-purpose flour
1½ cups whole wheat flour

Dissolve the yeast in the water. Add the salt and sugar and stir to combine.

Add 1 cup of the white flour and 1 cup of the whole wheat flour. Stir well. Continue stirring in flour 1 cup at a time until the dough is stiff and forms a rough ball.

Turn the dough onto a floured surface. Knead the dough, adding flour as needed, until the dough is no longer sticky, about 10 to 15 minutes. Knead rhythmically, repeating a pattern of pushing, turning, and folding the dough. The dough should be soft and elastic, springing back slightly when pinched.

Oil a bowl. Put the dough in the bowl, turning it to coat it all over with oil. Cover the bowl with plastic wrap or a towel and let the dough rise until it has doubled in size, about 2 hours.

You can let the dough rise in loaf pans, on a sheet pan, or in bread rising baskets. If you use bread pans or sheet pans, oil or butter them to keep the dough from sticking. If you use rising baskets, simply flour them.

Punch down the dough. Divide it in two and shape the loaves. Place the loaves in the prepared pans. Cover the dough and let it rise until it has doubled again, about 1½ to 2 hours.

Preheat the oven to 425 degrees about 45 minutes to an hour before you want to bake. If you are using a baking stone, place it in the oven when you turn it on so that it is heated through before you start baking.

Bake the loaves for 30 minutes, checking them after 20 minutes. Turn the loaves if they are browning unevenly. Bread is done when the loaves are well browned and sound hollow when tapped on the bottom. If the loaf feels soft or sounds dense when tapped, return it to the oven and bake it for another 5 minutes.

Potato Rye Bread

This bread is a great way to use leftover mashed potatoes. Or, you can cook one russet potato and mash it to make this light, flavorful bread. We sometimes add caraway or fennel seeds to the dough.
// **MAKES 2 LOAVES**

2 teaspoons active dry yeast
2 cups warm water (about 75 degrees)
1 cup mashed potatoes
1 tablespoon sugar or honey

1 tablespoon salt
1 cup rye flour
1 cup whole wheat flour
3½ to 4 cups unbleached bread or all-purpose flour

Dissolve the yeast in the water. Add the mashed potatoes, sugar, salt, rye flour, and whole wheat flour. Stir well. Continue stirring and adding flour 1 cup at a time until the dough is stiff and forms a rough ball.

Turn the dough onto a floured surface. Knead the dough, adding flour as needed, until it is no longer sticky, about 10 to 15 minutes. The dough should be soft and elastic. Don't worry if small pieces of potato remain; they will incorporate into the dough.

Oil a bowl. Put the dough in the bowl, turning to coat it all over with oil. Cover the bowl with plastic wrap or a towel and let the dough rise until it has doubled, about 2 hours.

Prepare your pans. Turn the dough out of the bowl, divide it in half, and shape the loaves. Place the loaves in the prepared pans and cover them. Let the dough rise until it has doubled again, about 1½ to 2 hours.

Preheat the oven to 425 degrees about 45 minutes to an hour before you want to bake. If you are using a baking stone, place it in the oven when you turn it on so that it is heated through before you start baking.

Bake the loaves for 30 minutes. Check the loaves after 20 minutes, and turn them if they are baking unevenly.

Oatmeal Bread

You can make this bread with rolled oats that you have soaked, or you can make it with leftover oatmeal. The quantity of flour needed may vary depending on the quantity and consistency of the oatmeal.
// MAKES 2 LOAVES

2½ cups water
1 cup rolled oats
2 teaspoons active dry yeast
1 tablespoon salt

1 tablespoon sugar or honey
4 cups unbleached bread or all-purpose flour
1 cup whole wheat flour

Bring 2 cups of the water to a boil. Put the rolled oats in a large bowl and pour the boiling water over them. Let the oats soak for 30 minutes, or until cooled.

Dissolve the yeast in ½ cup of warm (about 75 degrees) water. Add the salt and sugar and stir to combine. Add the yeast mixture to the oat mixture.

Add 1 cup of white flour and the whole wheat flour. Stir well. Continue stirring in flour 1 cup at a time until the dough is stiff and forms a rough ball.

Turn the dough onto a floured surface. Knead the dough, adding flour as needed, until the dough is no longer sticky, about 10 to 15 minutes. Knead rhythmically, repeating a pattern of pushing, turning, and folding the dough. The dough should be soft and elastic, springing back slightly when pinched.

Oil a bowl. Put the dough in the bowl, turning to coat it all over with oil. Cover the bowl with plastic wrap or a towel and let the dough rise until it has doubled, about 2 hours.

You can let the dough rise in loaf pans, on a sheet pan, or in bread rising baskets. If you use bread pans or sheet pans, oil or butter them to keep the dough from sticking. If you use rising baskets, simply flour them.

Punch down the dough. Divide it in two and shape the loaves. Place the loaves in the prepared pans or rising baskets or set the formed loaves on a sheet pan dusted with cornmeal. Cover the dough and let it rise until it has doubled again, about 1½ to 2 hours.

Preheat the oven to 425 degrees about 45 minutes to an hour before you want to bake. If you are using a baking stone, place it in the oven when you turn it on so that it is heated through before you start baking.

Bake the loaves for 30 minutes, checking them after 20 minutes. Turn the loaves if they are browning unevenly. Bread is done when the loaves are well browned and sound hollow when tapped on the bottom. If the loaf feels soft or sounds dense when tapped, return it to the oven and bake it for another 5 minutes.

Cinnamon Swirl Bread

This is a variation of our Whole Wheat Bread recipe. A swirl of cinnamon and sugar creates a sweet, fragrant breakfast loaf. You could also make it with raisins and nuts. Simply spread the nuts and raisins on the dough along with the cinnamon sugar. // **MAKES 2 LOAVES**

BREAD //
2 teaspoons active dry yeast
2 cups warm water (about 75 degrees)
1 tablespoon salt
1 tablespoon sugar or honey
4½ cups unbleached bread or all-purpose flour
1½ cups whole wheat flour

FILLING //
⅓ cup sugar
1½ teaspoons ground cinnamon
1 tablespoon butter, melted

Dissolve the yeast in the water. Add the salt and sugar and stir to combine.

Add 1 cup of white flour and 1 cup of whole wheat flour. Stir well. Continue stirring in flour 1 cup at a time until the dough is stiff and forms a rough ball.

Turn the dough onto a floured surface. Knead the dough, adding flour as needed, until the dough is no longer sticky, about 10 to 15 minutes. Knead rhythmically, repeating a pattern of pushing, turning, and folding the dough. The dough should be soft and elastic, springing back slightly when pinched.

Oil a bowl. Put the dough in the bowl, turning to coat it all over with oil. Cover the bowl with plastic wrap or a towel and let the dough rise until it has doubled, about 2 hours.

Thoroughly grease two loaf pans with oil or butter to prevent the dough from sticking.

Combine the sugar with the cinnamon to make the filling.

Punch down the dough, and divide it into two equal pieces. Working with one piece at a time, roll the dough into a rectangle approximately 12 by 8 inches. Brush the dough with half of the melted butter, leaving a border along the short side of the dough, which is where the seam will be. Sprinkle half of the cinnamon sugar on the buttered dough. Roll tightly from the short side. Seal the edges firmly, or they might come unsealed. Repeat with the remaining piece of dough.

Place the loaves seam-side down in the prepared loaf pans. Cover the dough and let it rise until it has doubled again, about 1½ to 2 hours. If a loaf comes unsealed, gently pinch the sides together again to seal them.

Preheat the oven to 425 degrees about 45 minutes to an hour before you want to bake.

Bake the loaves for 30 minutes, checking them after 20 minutes. Turn the loaves if they are browning unevenly. Bread is done when the loaves are well browned and sound hollow when tapped on the bottom. If the loaf feels soft or sounds dense when tapped, return it to the oven and bake it for another 5 minutes.

Let the bread cool completely before slicing it.

Dinner Rolls

Any yeast dough can be made into rolls, but this recipe bakes into a light, golden roll with a soft crust that will go with any meal. Adding a little whole wheat flour or whole wheat pastry flour will change the texture and create a heartier roll. For a soft roll, make the dough with unbleached all-purpose flour. **// MAKES 16 ROLLS**

1 tablespoon active dry yeast
¼ cup warm water (about 75 degrees)
1 medium white potato, cooked and mashed (½ cup)
1 egg, at room temperature and lightly beaten
½ cup milk, at room temperature

3 tablespoons honey or sugar
5 tablespoons unsalted butter, at room temperature
½ teaspoon salt
3 to 3½ cups unbleached flour or a combination of
    white and whole wheat flours

Dissolve the yeast in the warm water in a large mixing bowl. Add the mashed potato, egg, milk, honey, butter, and salt. Stir to combine. Add 1 cup of flour and stir well. Add another cup of flour and stir until you have a smooth batter. Continue adding flour a little at a time until the dough is stiff and holding together.

Turn the dough onto a floured surface. Knead, adding flour as needed, until the dough is soft and pliable and no longer sticky.

Place the dough in an oiled bowl and turn it to coat the dough with oil. Cover the bowl with a towel and place the dough in a warm, draft-free location to rise. Let the dough rise until it has doubled in size, about 1 to 1½ hours. Punch down the dough and divide it in half.

Roll each piece of dough into a rope shape, and then cut each one into eight pieces. Shape each piece of dough into a ball. Arrange them in 8- or 9-inch oiled cake pans.

Cover the pan with a towel and place it in a warm, draft-free location. Let the dough rise until it has doubled again, about 30 minutes.

Preheat the oven to 400 degrees.

Bake the rolls until they are golden brown, about 12 to 15 minutes. Place them on a rack to cool.

quick breads

QUICK BREADS are just that, quick to make.
They are leavened with baking powder, baking soda, or both,
so the dough doesn't have to rise before baking.

Banana Wheat Germ Bread

Did we all grow up on banana bread? It seems that here in the Midwest, everyone's mom made delicious bread with ripe bananas. This hearty recipe is nutritious and moist. For a lighter loaf, eliminate the whole wheat flour and use 3 cups of unbleached all-purpose flour. // **MAKES 2 LOAVES**

1 cup butter, at room temperature
⅔ cup honey or sugar
4 eggs, slightly beaten
½ cup buttermilk
2 teaspoons vanilla
6 very ripe bananas, mashed
1 teaspoon baking soda
1 tablespoon baking powder

½ teaspoon salt
2 cups whole wheat pastry flour
1 cup unbleached all-purpose flour
1 cup wheat germ
1 teaspoon cinnamon
1 cup chopped walnuts or pecans
1 cup unsweetened coconut (optional)

Preheat the oven to 350 degrees, and butter two loaf pans.

Cream the butter. Add the honey and beat until creamy. Add the eggs one at a time, beating well after each addition. Add the buttermilk, vanilla, and bananas, and stir to combine.

Combine the baking soda, baking powder, salt, flour, wheat germ, and cinnamon in a bowl. Add the dry ingredients to the wet ingredients, and stir until well mixed. Add the nuts and coconut (if using). Pour the batter into the prepared loaf pans.

Bake for 60 to 70 minutes. Test the loaves with a cake tester. It should come out clean. Let the loaves cool in the pans for 10 to 15 minutes, and then turn the loaves out onto a rack. Let the bread cool completely before slicing it.

This recipe can also be made into muffins. A half recipe will make 12 muffins. Bake muffins for 20 minutes.

Coconut Orange Bread

This tropical-tasting bread makes us think we're in a faraway land with the ocean at our feet! The coconut creates a very moist and deliciously chewy loaf. // **MAKES 1 LOAF**

3 tablespoons butter
½ cup honey or sugar
2 eggs
1 teaspoon vanilla
¼ cup fresh orange juice

2 cups flour
1 tablespoon baking powder
¼ teaspoon salt
½ cup unsweetened coconut
1 tablespoon grated orange zest (optional)

Preheat the oven to 350 degrees, and butter a loaf pan.

Cream the butter. Beat in the honey until the mixture is smooth and creamy. Add the eggs and beat until they are incorporated. Beat in the vanilla and orange juice.

Combine the flour, baking powder, and salt. Stir the dry ingredients into the wet ingredients. Fold in the coconut and orange zest (if using). Pour the batter into the prepared loaf pan.

Bake the bread for 45 to 50 minutes. The bread is done when a cake tester inserted in the center comes out clean. Let the loaf cool for 10 to 15 minutes; then turn it out onto a rack. Cool the bread completely on the rack before slicing it.

Pumpkin Bread

This bread is equally good when you substitute sweet potato or winter squash for the pumpkin.
// MAKES 2 LOAVES

¾ cup vegetable oil

¾ cup sugar

3 eggs

2 cups pureed cooked pumpkin

1½ cups whole wheat flour

2 cups unbleached all-purpose flour

1 teaspoon baking powder

2 teaspoons baking soda

1 teaspoon salt

2 teaspoons cinnamon

½ teaspoon ground allspice

¼ teaspoon ground cloves

1 cup chopped walnuts or pecans (optional)

Preheat the oven to 350 degrees, and butter two loaf pans. If you are using glass loaf pans, preheat the oven to 325 degrees.

Beat the oil and sugar until light and creamy. Add the eggs and pumpkin. Beat until well combined.

Combine the flour, baking powder, baking soda, salt, cinnamon, allspice, and cloves in a bowl. Gradually stir the dry ingredients into the pumpkin mixture. Continue stirring until they are completely incorporated. Add the nuts (if using). Spoon the mixture into the prepared loaf pans.

Bake the bread for 50 minutes to 1 hour. The bread is done when a cake tester inserted in the center comes out clean. Let the loaves cool for 10 to 15 minutes, and then turn them out onto a rack. Let the bread cool completely before slicing it.

Date Nut Bread

Dates are a good high-energy food. They contain 54 percent sugar and 7 percent protein when they are fresh and higher concentrations when they are dried. This bread is moist and sweet, making it a great breakfast or tea loaf. // **MAKES 2 LOAVES**

2 cups chopped pitted dates
2 cups boiling water
3 cups unbleached all-purpose flour (use part whole
    wheat flour or whole wheat pastry flour, if desired)
1 teaspoon salt
1 teaspoon baking soda

½ cup butter, at room temperature
1½ cups brown sugar
2 eggs
1 teaspoon vanilla
1 cup chopped walnuts or pecans
Grated zest of 1 orange (optional)

Preheat the oven to 350 degrees, and butter two loaf pans. If you are using glass pans, preheat the oven to 325 degrees instead.

Combine the dates and boiling water in a bowl. Set the dates aside to cool to room temperature.

Combine the flour, salt, and baking soda in a small bowl.

In another bowl, beat the butter and sugar until creamy. Add the eggs one at a time, beating well after each addition. Stir in the vanilla.

Add the dry ingredients and stir just until incorporated. Stir in the date mixture, nuts, and orange zest (if using). Distribute the batter evenly between the two prepared loaf pans.

Bake the bread for 50 to 60 minutes. The bread is done when a toothpick or a cake tester pushed into the center of the bread comes out clean. Let the loaves cool for 10 to 15 minutes, and then turn them out onto a rack. Cool the bread completely before slicing it.

Apricot Bread

This is a sweet, spicy loaf that goes well with afternoon tea or Sunday brunch. You can use whole wheat pastry flour in place of some of the white flour for a heartier texture. This bread is nice in the morning, toasted and accompanied by thick yogurt or cream cheese. // **MAKES 1 LOAF**

½ cup boiling water
1 cup dried apricots, chopped
2 tablespoons butter
½ cup sugar
1 egg, slightly beaten
1 cup plain yogurt
½ cup rolled oats
2 cups unbleached all-purpose flour

1 tablespoon baking powder
½ teaspoon baking soda
½ teaspoon salt
¼ teaspoon nutmeg
¼ teaspoon ginger
½ cup pecans, chopped
2 teaspoons grated orange zest (optional)

Preheat the oven to 350 degrees, and butter a loaf pan.

Pour the boiling water over the chopped apricots, and let it sit while you prepare the batter.

In a large bowl, cream the butter. Add the sugar and beat until well blended. Add the egg and the yogurt and mix well.

In a separate bowl, combine the oats, flour, baking powder, baking soda, salt, nutmeg, and ginger. Stir the dry ingredients into the wet mixture. Drain the apricots well and fold them into the batter along with the nuts and orange rind (if using). Pour the batter into the prepared loaf pan.

Bake the bread for 45 to 50 minutes. The bread is done when a cake tester inserted in the middle comes out clean. Let the loaf cool for 10 to 15 minutes, and then turn it out onto a rack. Let the bread cool completely before slicing it.

Cranberry Bread

Cranberries are harvested in the fall and are available fresh in the markets through the holidays and early winter months. We like to freeze them for use in breads and cakes throughout the winter. Here is our version of the traditional cranberry sweet bread. It is as pretty as it is delicious. This is a dense, sweet bread; for a lighter version, use part or all unbleached all-purpose flour. **// MAKES 1 LOAF**

¼ cup butter, at room temperature
½ cup honey or sugar
1 egg, slightly beaten
1 cup orange juice
2 tablespoons grated orange zest
2 cups whole wheat flour

2 teaspoons baking powder
½ teaspoon baking soda
½ teaspoon salt
½ cup chopped walnuts or pecans
1 cup cranberries, coarsely chopped

Preheat the oven to 350 degrees, and butter a loaf pan. If you are using a glass loaf pan, preheat the oven to 325 degrees instead.

Cream the butter. Add the honey and beat until the mixture is light and creamy. Add the egg, orange juice, and orange zest, beating until well mixed.

Combine the flour, baking powder, baking soda, and salt. Stir the dry ingredients into the wet ingredients just until combined. Stir in the nuts and cranberries. Pour the batter into the prepared loaf pan.

Bake for 50 minutes to 1 hour. The bread is done when a cake tester inserted in the middle comes out clean. Let the bread cool for 10 to 15 minutes, and then turn it out onto a cooling rack. Cool the bread completely before slicing it.

Scones with Dried Fruit

Scones are an easy morning treat. This recipe calls for currants, but any dried fruit will work. The dough is essentially biscuit dough and should be treated as gently as possible. Stir in the buttermilk until just mixed, and resist the temptation to add more liquid if the dough seems dry. You will be rewarded with a light, flaky scone. Enjoy! // **MAKES 8 SCONES**

⅓ cup currants
2 cups unbleached all-purpose flour or 1¾ cups all-purpose and ¼ cup whole wheat pastry flour
⅓ cup sugar
2 teaspoons baking powder

½ teaspoon baking soda
¼ teaspoon salt
½ teaspoon cinnamon
½ cup cold unsalted butter
¾ cup buttermilk

Preheat the oven to 375 degrees.

If the fruit seems really dry or hard, soak it in a little hot water while you assemble the rest of the ingredients. Drain well before adding the fruit to the dough.

Whisk together the flour, sugar, baking powder, baking soda, salt, and cinnamon in a bowl.

Cut the butter into small pieces. Add the butter to the dry ingredients, and cut it in with a pastry blender. (You can also do this in a food processor. Pulse until well incorporated and then transfer the mixture to a bowl.)

Gently stir in the buttermilk and currants. The dough may seem dry. Do not be tempted to add more buttermilk. Turn the dough onto a floured surface. Place any flour that is left in the bottom of your bowl on top of the dough. Push the mixture together into a ball, gathering in any pieces that have fallen off. Gently push the dough into an 8-inch round. Cut the round in half, then into quarters, and then eighths. You should have 8 equal wedges.

Place the scones on a cookie sheet. Bake for 10 to 12 minutes, until the scones are lightly browned. The scones are done if they bounce back when you push on the top.

Transfer the scones from the baking sheet to a cooling rack. Serve warm.

Variations

Try these ingredients instead of currants, or make up your own combinations:

dried cranberries and orange zest
dried tart cherries and lemon zest
dried prunes
dried apricots and almonds
dried apples and pecans

Lemon Blueberry Muffins

This is a sweet muffin made with yogurt, which gives it a slight tang and a light, tender texture. These muffins are delicious for a midmorning snack or Sunday brunch. **// MAKES 12 LARGE MUFFINS**

3 cups unbleached all-purpose flour
2 teaspoons baking powder
½ teaspoon baking soda
½ teaspoon salt
5 tablespoons unsalted butter, softened
¼ cup vegetable oil

¾ cup sugar
1 tablespoon grated lemon zest
2 eggs
1½ cups low-fat plain yogurt
6 ounces (1½ cups) fresh blueberries

Preheat the oven to 375 degrees. Grease a 12-cup muffin tin with butter or line it with paper baking cups.

Whisk together the flour, baking powder, baking soda, and salt in a bowl and set it aside.

In another bowl, cream the butter, oil, sugar, and lemon zest with an electric mixer until the mixture is light and fluffy. Add the eggs one at a time, beating well after each addition. Beat in half of the dry ingredients. Add one-third of the yogurt. Beat in the remaining dry ingredients in two batches, alternating with the yogurt, until the batter is well blended. Fold in the blueberries.

Divide the batter evenly among the cups in the muffin tin.

Bake until the muffins are golden brown, about 20 to 25 minutes. Place the pan on a wire rack to cool for 5 minutes. Remove the muffins from the tin and serve them warm.

Lemon Blueberry Muffins

Pecan Coffee Cake

This is a recipe for a classic coffee cake layered with cinnamon-pecan streusel. Combining the baking soda and yogurt and allowing it to proof gives the soda more leavening power, which creates a rich, moist cake. You can also make this coffee cake in a 9 × 13-inch cake pan: put the streusel on top and use a knife to swirl it in. **// SERVES 10 TO 12**

1½ cups plain yogurt or sour cream
2 teaspoons baking soda
1 cup pecans, coarsely chopped
2 teaspoons cinnamon
3 tablespoons date sugar (available at natural food stores)
3 cups unbleached all-purpose flour

2 teaspoons baking powder
1½ teaspoons salt
4 tablespoons butter, at room temperature
1 cup honey
3 eggs
1 tablespoon vanilla

Preheat the oven to 350 degrees, and butter a 12-cup Bundt pan or tube pan.

Blend the yogurt and the baking soda. Cover and let stand at room temperature for 30 minutes.

Mix the pecans with the cinnamon and date sugar. Set the streusel aside.

Combine the flour, baking powder, and salt. Set the dry ingredients aside.

In another bowl, beat the butter until it is smooth. Add the honey and beat until well blended. Add the eggs, vanilla, and yogurt mixture. Beat well. Add the dry ingredients and stir just until combined. Do not overbeat.

Cover the bottom of the prepared pan with a thin layer of batter. Sprinkle half of the streusel over the batter. Add another thin layer of batter and then the rest of the streusel. Pour the remaining batter into the pan and smooth the top with a spoon or spatula.

Bake the cake until a cake tester comes out clean, approximately 45 minutes. Set the pan on a wire cooling rack, and let the cake cool in the pan for 5 to 10 minutes. Invert the pan on the rack and tap to remove the cake from the pan. Let the cake cool before slicing it.

French Toast

Instead of cream or milk, we use coconut milk, which makes for exotic-tasting French toast. This is great made with French bread or light whole wheat bread. // **SERVES 3**

¼ teaspoon cinnamon
¼ teaspoon cardamom
Grated zest of 1 lime
2 teaspoons lime juice

1 cup light coconut milk
2 eggs
¼ teaspoon salt
9 to 10 slices of bread

Combine all of the ingredients except the bread in a bowl large enough to dip the bread into. Beat with a small whisk or a fork until the eggs are well beaten.

Preheat a griddle or a large skillet until it is hot, and then lower the temperature to medium. Lightly butter the griddle. Dip the bread into the batter, and cook the toast until it is golden brown on both sides.

Variation

French Toast with Rose Water and Cardamom

In this variation, rose water replaces the cinnamon and lime. Follow the directions given in the main recipe.

2 teaspoons rose water
¼ teaspoon cardamom
1 cup light coconut milk
2 eggs
¼ teaspoon salt

Buttermilk Cornbread

This cornbread is rich and moist. It is best eaten fresh out of the oven. Serve it with black bean chili or stewed pinto beans. This recipe can be easily divided in half and made in a 9-inch square pan.
// **SERVES 10 TO 12**

4 eggs
2 cups buttermilk
¼ to ⅓ cup honey or sugar
½ cup vegetable oil
1 cup unbleached all-purpose flour

2½ teaspoons baking powder
1 teaspoon baking soda
½ teaspoon salt
2½ cups coarse cornmeal (available at food co-ops and
    natural food stores)

Preheat the oven to 350 degrees, and oil a 9 × 13-inch pan.

In a mixing bowl, beat the eggs until they are light. Add the buttermilk, honey (use ⅓ cup if you prefer sweet cornbread), and oil. Stir to combine.

In a separate bowl, combine the flour, baking powder, baking soda, salt, and cornmeal. Stir the dry ingredients into the wet mixture, and continue stirring until smooth.

Pour the batter into the prepared pan and spread it evenly. Bake for 30 to 35 minutes. When it is done, the cornbread will spring back when touched lightly in the center. Or test it with a toothpick or a cake tester.

Set the pan on a wire rack to cool for about 10 minutes. Serve the cornbread warm.

desserts

Carrot Cake with Cream Cheese Frosting

This is a lighter-than-typical carrot cake. Using currants instead of raisins makes it easier to cut. The cake is paired with a light cream cheese frosting (the secret to the light frosting is whipped cream). Use organic cream cheese if you can; it's a very nice product. You can add cocoa powder for a chocolate frosting; just sweeten it up a little more to compensate. A little booze can be a nice addition too. Walnuts make a great garnish on top. // **SERVES 10 TO 12**

CAKE //

3 eggs
⅓ cup vegetable oil
⅔ cup buttermilk, at room temperature
⅓ cup sugar
½ cup honey
2 teaspoons vanilla
2 cups unbleached all-purpose flour
2 teaspoons baking powder
1 teaspoon baking soda
1 teaspoon salt
1½ teaspoons cinnamon
Grated fresh nutmeg (optional)
1½ cups slightly packed grated carrots
½ cup unsweetened shredded coconut
⅓ cup currants or raisins

CREAM CHEESE FROSTING //

¾ pound cream cheese, at room temperature
6 tablespoons butter, at room temperature
⅓ cup honey or maple syrup
⅓ cup powdered sugar
Zest of half a lemon
Pinch of salt
1 cup heavy cream

Preheat the oven to 350 degrees. Butter and flour two 9-inch cake pans or one 9 × 13-inch pan.

Beat the eggs. Stir in the oil, buttermilk, sugar, honey, and vanilla.

In another bowl, whisk together the flour, baking powder, baking soda, salt, cinnamon, and nutmeg (if using). Add the dry ingredients in thirds, alternating with the carrots.

Stir gently after each addition just until the ingredients are all incorporated. Adding the carrots in three batches makes the carrots less likely to clump, so you can avoid stirring too vigorously. This cake is best when the batter is handled gently. Do not overbeat.

Add the coconut and currants with the last addition of carrots. Pour the batter into the prepared pans and smooth the top. Bake for 25 to 30 minutes. Cakes made in a single large pan will take longer to bake. If you are making a layer cake, cool the cake in the pans for about 10 minutes; then invert and remove the pans. Cool the cake completely before frosting it.

Carrot Cake with Cream Cheese Frosting

Cream together the cream cheese, butter, and honey. Add the powdered sugar, lemon zest, and salt and mix well.

In another bowl, whip the cream until it is a stiff consistency. You want to go past the point of soft peaks, but not so far as to make butter. Fold the whipped cream into the frosting.

Note: Powdered sugar makes a frosting stiff. For softer frosting, omit the powdered sugar and increase the honey to ⅔ cup.

Almond Cake with Whipped Cream and Berries

This is a very delicious and versatile cake. We serve it layered with a variety of different fillings: berries and whipped cream, raspberry preserves, chocolate ganache, or orange marmalade lightened with whipped cream, to name just a few. This cake is also a delightful base for strawberry shortcake. // **SERVES 10 TO 12**

Almond Cake with Whipped Cream and Berries

½ cup butter

1 cup sugar

3 eggs, separated, plus 1 additional egg white

½ cup plain yogurt

½ teaspoon almond extract

1 cup unbleached all-purpose flour

1½ cups ground almonds

1½ teaspoons baking soda

1½ teaspoons baking powder

½ teaspoon salt

Preheat the oven to 350 degrees. Lightly butter and flour two 9-inch cake pans or one 9 × 13-inch pan.

Cream the butter. Add the sugar and beat until creamy. Add the egg yolks, yogurt, and almond extract. Beat until well blended.

Whisk together the flour, ground almonds, baking soda, baking powder, and salt in a separate bowl. Stir the dry ingredients into the butter mixture.

Whip the egg whites until they are stiff. Using a rubber spatula, gently fold the egg whites into the batter. Pour the batter into the prepared pans.

Bake the cake for 25 to 30 minutes. The cake is done when a cake tester inserted in the center comes out clean. Cakes made in a single large pan will take longer to bake. If you are making a layer cake, cool the cake in the pans for about 10 minutes; then invert and remove the pans. Cool the cake completely before frosting it.

Cardamom Spice Cake

Cardamom is a very fragrant spice that is much more flavorful when ground just before using it. You can buy the cardamom pods wherever fresh herbs and spices are sold. Roll the pods between your fingers and they will easily open, exposing several small seeds. Crush the seeds in a mortar and pestle. // **SERVES 8 TO 10**

1 cup unbleached all-purpose flour
½ teaspoon baking powder
½ teaspoon baking soda
¼ teaspoon salt
¼ teaspoon ground cloves
½ teaspoon ground cinnamon

¼ teaspoon freshly ground cardamom
4 tablespoons unsalted butter
¾ cup honey
1 egg
½ teaspoon vanilla
½ cup buttermilk

Preheat the oven to 350 degrees. Butter and flour an 8-inch cake pan; either square or round is fine.

Whisk together the flour, baking powder, baking soda, salt, cloves, cinnamon, and cardamom in a bowl.

In another bowl, cream the butter with a mixer. Add the honey and beat again until the honey is incorporated. Beat in the egg and vanilla. Add the dry ingredients in three batches, alternating with the buttermilk and beating after each addition, until all of the ingredients have been incorporated. Pour the cake batter into the prepared pan.

Bake until the center of the cake is set and a cake tester comes out clean, about 25 to 30 minutes. Cool the cake in the pan for about 10 minutes; then invert and remove the pan.

Mango Cake

This is a very versatile cake recipe. Mango has an exotic tropical flavor and adds great color. We like to pair it with lime, coconut, or both. You can also substitute chopped apple or rhubarb for the mango in this recipe. When using apple or rhubarb, you may want to add nuts as well. Serve the cake topped with cream cheese frosting (page 219) made with lime instead of lemon or serve with whipped cream and fresh fruit. // **SERVES 10 TO 12**

½ cup butter, at room temperature
¾ cup honey
2 eggs, lightly beaten
1 teaspoon vanilla
½ cup plain yogurt
2 cups unbleached all-purpose flour
½ teaspoon salt

2 teaspoons baking soda
½ teaspoon ground cinnamon
¼ teaspoon ground allspice
2 mangos, chopped (2 cups)
½ cup chopped nuts or unsweetened shredded
  coconut (optional)

Preheat the oven to 350 degrees. Butter and flour two 9-inch cake pans or one 13 × 9-inch pan.

Cream the butter; then add the honey and continue beating until well mixed. Beat in the eggs, vanilla, and yogurt.

Combine the flour, salt, baking soda, cinnamon, and all-spice in a separate bowl. Stir the dry ingredients into the wet ingredients until well blended. Add the mango and the nuts or coconut (if using), and stir just until incorporated.

Pour the cake batter into the prepared pans and smooth the top. Bake for 25 to 30 minutes. The cake is done when a cake tester comes out clean or the top springs back when you lightly press it. Cakes made in a single large pan will take longer to bake. If you are making a layer cake, cool the cake in the pans for about 10 minutes; then invert and remove the pans. Cool the cake completely before frosting it.

Apple Walnut Cake

This is a very versatile cake recipe. Try rhubarb instead of apples, or use a combination of the two. This cake is great with salted caramel sauce or served with a little whipped cream or ice cream. It's delicious for brunch or tea as well as dessert. **// SERVES 10 TO 12**

½ cup butter
1 cup honey or sugar
2 eggs, beaten
1 teaspoon vanilla
½ cup plain yogurt
2 cups unbleached all-purpose flour or 1 cup whole wheat
    pastry and 1 cup unbleached all-purpose flour

½ teaspoon salt
2 teaspoons baking soda
1 teaspoon cinnamon
½ teaspoon allspice
3 medium apples, peeled, cored, and cut into
    ¼-inch pieces (3 cups)
½ cup walnuts, chopped

Preheat the oven to 350 degrees. Butter and flour two 9-inch cake pans or one 13 × 9-inch pan.

Cream the butter. Add the honey and beat until creamy. Add the eggs, vanilla, and yogurt. Beat until well blended.

Combine the flour, salt, baking soda, cinnamon, and allspice in a separate bowl. Add the dry ingredients to the butter mixture, beating until fully incorporated. Stir in the apples and walnuts. Pour the batter into the prepared pans.

Bake the cake for 30 to 35 minutes. The cake is done when a cake tester inserted in the middle comes out clean. Cakes made in a single large pan will take longer to bake. Cool the cake on a wire rack. If you are making a layer cake, invert the pans and remove the cake after 10 minutes of cooling.

Ames Farm primarily grows apples developed by the University of Minnesota Horticulture Research Center.

Applesauce Cake

This is a simple cake for tea time or the lunchbox and a great cake to take along on a picnic or a road trip. It does not need any icing, but you could sprinkle it with powdered sugar or serve it with a dollop of whipped cream or ice cream. **// SERVES 8 TO 10**

1¼ cups unbleached all-purpose flour or a mixture of
    all-purpose flour and whole wheat pastry flour
1 teaspoon baking powder
½ teaspoon baking soda
½ teaspoon salt
½ teaspoon ground cinnamon
¼ teaspoon ground nutmeg

4 tablespoons butter, softened
1 cup sugar
1 egg
¾ cup unsweetened applesauce
½ cup chopped cranberries or raisins
½ cup chopped pecans or walnuts (optional)

Preheat the oven to 350 degrees. Lightly oil an 8- or 9-inch cake pan, either square or round.

Sift together the flour, baking powder, baking soda, salt, cinnamon, and nutmeg.

In a separate bowl, beat the butter and sugar until creamy. Beat in the egg. Add half of the dry ingredients and stir until well combined. Then stir in half of the applesauce. Add the rest of the dry ingredients followed by the rest of the applesauce, mixing well after each addition. Fold in the cranberries and nuts (if using).

Spoon the batter into the prepared pan, spreading it evenly.

Bake for 25 to 30 minutes until the cake is light brown and a cake tester inserted in the center of the cake comes out clean. Cool the cake on a wire rack for 10 minutes. Then invert the pan to remove the cake. Cool the cake completely before slicing it.

Pumpkin Cake

You can make pumpkin cake with winter squash or sweet potatoes instead of fresh pureed pumpkin. Canned pumpkin is easy and has a great texture. Whole wheat pastry flour adds some fiber and gives the cake a denser texture. We like to use half whole wheat and half unbleached all-purpose flour. Top the cake with cream cheese frosting (page 219) or a simple dusting of powdered sugar. // **SERVES 10 TO 12**

½ cup vegetable oil

¾ cup lightly packed brown sugar or honey

2 eggs, lightly beaten

1 teaspoon vanilla

½ cup plain yogurt

2 cups pumpkin puree or 1 (15-ounce) can pumpkin

2 cups unbleached all-purpose flour or a mixture of all-purpose flour and whole wheat pastry flour

½ teaspoon salt

2 teaspoons baking soda

½ teaspoon ground cinnamon

½ teaspoon ground allspice

½ cup chopped walnuts or pecans

Preheat the oven to 350 degrees. Butter and flour two 9-inch cake pans or one 9 × 13-inch pan.

Combine the oil and brown sugar. Add the eggs, vanilla, yogurt, and pumpkin and mix well.

Combine the flour, salt, baking soda, cinnamon, and allspice in a separate bowl. Stir the dry ingredients into the wet ingredients. Stir in the nuts, mixing until just combined. Pour the cake batter into the prepared pans and smooth the top.

Pie pumpkins are smaller and sweeter and have a smoother texture than field pumpkins. Cinderella is a popular pie pumpkin.

Bake the cake for 25 to 30 minutes. The cake is done when a cake tester comes out clean or the top springs back after you lightly press it. Cakes made in a single large pan will take longer to bake. Cool the cake on a wire rack. If you are making a layer cake, invert the pans and remove the cake after 10 minutes of cooling.

Note: To make pumpkin puree, cut a pie pumpkin in half and scoop out the seeds. Toast the pumpkin cut-side up in a 350 degree oven until it is soft, about 1½ hours. Let the pumpkin cool; then scoop out and mash the flesh. You will get about 4 cups of puree from a 5-pound pumpkin. Freeze the leftover puree.

Pear Upside-Down Cake

This is a quick cake to assemble. It can be served as an evening dessert or as a breakfast cake. We also make this recipe using peaches in place of the pears. The cake is moist and best served the day it is made. It stands alone quite well, but if you want to make it special, a little whipped cream or crème fraîche is wonderful. // **SERVES 8**

½ cup plus 3 tablespoons unsalted butter,
    at room temperature
¾ cup plus ⅓ cup sugar
2 tablespoons brown sugar
3 medium pears, peeled, cored, and sliced
1½ cups unbleached all-purpose flour
1 teaspoon baking powder

1 teaspoon baking soda
¼ teaspoon salt
½ teaspoon cinnamon
1½ teaspoons vanilla
2 eggs, separated
½ cup buttermilk

Preheat the oven to 350 degrees.

Melt 3 tablespoons of the butter in a cast-iron skillet over medium heat. Add ⅓ cup of the sugar and all of the brown sugar. Stir until the sugar dissolves. Remove the pan from the heat. Arrange the pears in the pan. (If you use a traditional cake pan instead of the cast-iron skillet, melt the butter and sugars and transfer it to a cake pan. Arrange the fruit slices on top of the butter mixture.) Set the pan aside while you make the cake batter.

Whisk together the flour, baking powder, baking soda, salt, and cinnamon in a bowl.

Place the remaining ½ cup of butter and ¾ cup of sugar in a bowl and beat until creamy. Add the vanilla and egg yolks, and beat until well mixed. Add the flour mixture in thirds, alternating with the buttermilk, beating well after each addition.

In a separate bowl, beat the egg whites until they hold soft peaks. Gently fold the egg whites into the cake batter with a rubber spatula until they are completely incorporated. Spoon the batter onto the pears in the pan, being careful to cover them completely. Smooth gently.

Bake for 40 to 45 minutes. The cake will be golden brown and a cake tester will come out clean when the cake is done. Let the cake cool in the pan for 5 minutes, and then turn it over onto a cake plate. If any pears stick to the pan, simply transfer them to their place on the cake. Serve the cake warm or at room temperature.

Banana Coconut Cake

This is a heavy, moist cake. Serve it with honey-sweetened whipped cream or our light cream cheese frosting (page 219). // **SERVE 10 TO 12**

3 cups unbleached all-purpose flour
1 teaspoon baking soda
1 teaspoon ground cinnamon
½ teaspoon salt
1 cup vegetable oil
1¾ cups honey or 1½ cups sugar
2 teaspoons vanilla
3 eggs, separated
3 to 4 large bananas, mashed (2 cups)
1 cup golden raisins
1 cup walnuts, chopped
1 cup dried unsweetened coconut

Preheat the oven to 350 degrees. Butter and flour two 9-inch cake pans or one 9 × 13-inch pan.

Combine the flour, baking soda, cinnamon, and salt in a bowl.

Combine the oil, honey, and vanilla in another bowl and beat until well mixed. Add the egg yolks and beat until they are incorporated. Stir in the bananas, raisins, walnuts, and coconut. Add the flour mixture and stir well.

Ames Farm single-source honey is gathered from eighteen different locations during specific bloom times.

In a separate bowl, beat the egg whites until stiff. Gently fold the egg whites into the cake batter with a rubber spatula until well blended. Pour the batter into the prepared cake pans, dividing the batter equally between the two pans.

Bake for 30 to 40 minutes. Check for doneness after 30 minutes: a tester should come out clean and the top will spring back from a light touch. Cakes made in a single large pan will take longer to bake. Cool the cakes on a wire rack for 10 minutes. Then invert the pans to remove the cake layers. Let the cake cool completely before frosting it.

German Chocolate Cupcakes

This is one of those desserts that is hard to keep away from. It's a classic, delicious dessert that many of us remember from our childhoods. // **MAKES 12 CUPCAKES**

CUPCAKES//

1 cup unbleached all-purpose flour

½ cup cocoa

¾ teaspoon baking soda

¼ teaspoon salt

¼ cup butter

1 cup sugar

1 egg

1 teaspoon vanilla

¾ cup buttermilk, at room temperature

GERMAN COCONUT FROSTING//

¼ cup butter or virgin coconut oil

¼ cup honey

2 tablespoons maple syrup

1 egg

½ cup cream or soy milk

½ teaspoon vanilla

¾ cup unsweetened coconut flakes

½ cup chopped pecans or walnuts

Preheat the oven to 350 degrees. Line or oil and flour the cups of a 12-cup tin.

Combine the flour, cocoa, baking soda, and salt. Sift the dry ingredients or mix them well with a whisk to thoroughly incorporate the cocoa with the flour.

In a separate bowl, beat the butter and sugar. Add the egg and vanilla, and beat until the mixture is light and creamy.

Stir in ⅓ of the dry ingredients and then ⅓ of the buttermilk. Continue stirring in the ingredients, alternating between the dry ingredients and the buttermilk, until all of the ingredients have been incorporated. It is best to stir by hand or beat on low with a mixer. Do not overbeat.

Spoon the batter into the prepared muffin tin, filling the cups ⅔ full.

Bake for 20 minutes or until a cake tester comes out clean. Cool the cupcakes before frosting them. This recipe can also be made in a 9 × 13-inch cake pan; you'll need to adjust the baking time to about 30 minutes.

To make the frosting, combine the butter, honey, maple syrup, egg, and cream in a heavy-bottomed saucepan. Cook over medium heat, stirring, until thickened. Remove the pan from the heat. Stir in the vanilla, coconut, and nuts. Cool the frosting before spreading it on the cupcakes.

German Chocolate Cupcakes

Gingerbread

A traditional American dessert, gingerbread has long been a favorite at the cafe and is always a winner with children. We like to serve it with fruit sauce and a dollop of whipped cream. Gingerbread is very moist, making it a cake that keeps well. Serve it for brunch as well as for dessert. // **SERVES 10 TO 12**

1 cup butter, at room temperature
1 cup honey
¾ cup dark molasses (not blackstrap)
¾ cup boiling water
3 eggs

2¾ cups unbleached all-purpose flour
1 teaspoon salt
1½ teaspoons baking soda
1 teaspoon cinnamon
1 teaspoon ground ginger

Preheat the oven to 325 degrees. Butter a 9 × 13-inch pan or two 9-inch cake pans.

Cut the butter into small pieces and combine it with the honey and molasses in a large mixing bowl. Pour the boiling water into the bowl and stir until the butter melts. Allow it to cool.

Add the eggs to the cooled butter mixture and beat well.

Combine the flour, salt, baking soda, cinnamon, and ginger. Stir the dry ingredients into the wet mixture and beat until smooth. Pour the batter into the prepared pan.

Bake for 50 to 60 minutes or until a cake tester comes out clean, about. Cool on a wire rack.

Serve the gingerbread with sweetened whipped cream or with apple, pear, or strawberry sauce.

Tart Dough

This is a light and flaky tart dough that you can use for both sweet and savory tart recipes. The recipe makes enough dough to line an 8- or 9-inch tart pan. // **MAKES ONE 8- OR 9-INCH TART SHELL**

1¼ cups unbleached all-purpose flour
¼ teaspoon salt
5 tablespoons unsalted butter

1 egg
1 to 2 tablespoons ice water

Combine the flour and salt in a bowl. Cut the butter into small pieces and drop them into the flour. Work the butter into the flour with a pastry blender or two knives until the mixture resembles coarse meal.

In a small bowl, lightly beat the egg. Add 1 tablespoon of ice water and stir to combine. Slowly pour the egg mixture into the flour mixture while stirring with a fork. The mixture should be moist but not wet and should hold together in a ball. If the mixture seems too dry, add more water a little at a time until the dough comes together. Gather the dough into a ball. Flatten it into a disk and wrap it in plastic wrap. Refrigerate for 20 to 30 minutes.

Flour a work surface. Roll out the dough, starting from the center and moving toward the edges. Turn the dough and flour it as you go to prevent it from sticking. Roll until the tart dough is ⅛ inch thick. Carefully lay the dough in the tart pan.

Trim the excess dough, leaving about an inch beyond the edge of the pan. Fold in the extra dough and press it against the sides to double the thickness of the sides.

Chill the tart shell for at least one hour before prebaking or filling it.

To partially bake a tart shell, preheat the oven to 425 degrees. Line the shell with aluminum foil and fill it with dried beans, rice, or aluminum pellets. This keeps the sides from caving in and the bottom from bubbling up. Place the tart pan on the bottom shelf of the oven and bake for 15 minutes. Remove the pan from the oven, remove the weights and the foil, and return the shell to the oven for 5 more minutes to dry the bottom crust.

To bake a shell completely, follow the above steps but bake it for 20 minutes before removing the weights. Return the shell to the oven for an additional 5 minutes. The crust should be a light golden brown.

Pecan Tart

This is a great alternative to pecan pie at Thanksgiving. For chocolate lovers, add chocolate chips when you add the chopped nuts. // **SERVES 8**

3 tablespoons butter
1½ cups pecan halves
2 eggs
½ cup sugar

¼ cup maple syrup
1¼ teaspoons vanilla
⅛ teaspoon salt
1 partially baked 9-inch tart shell (page 233)

Preheat the oven to 350 degrees.

Melt the butter and set it aside to cool. Coarsely chop 1 cup of the nuts. Reserve the rest to decorate the top of the tart.

Beat the eggs. Add the sugar, maple syrup, vanilla, salt, and cooled butter. Beat until smooth. Stir in the chopped nuts.

Pour the mixture into the partially baked shell. Arrange the pecan halves on top. Bake for 30 to 35 minutes, or until the filling is just set but not dry.

Variation

For a chocolate pecan tart, add ½ cup of dark or semi-sweet chocolate chips when you add the chopped nuts.

Cranberry, Orange, Walnut Tart

This is a festive tart to serve for Thanksgiving, but is certainly welcome all fall and winter long. You can use fresh or frozen cranberries. There is no need to thaw frozen cranberries, and they are easier to chop when frozen. This is a very simple tart to make. If you have a tart shell already prepared, you can throw it together in just a few minutes. // SERVES 10 TO 12

2 eggs
½ cup honey or sugar
¼ cup butter, melted and cooled
2 tablespoons orange juice
1 teaspoon vanilla
¼ teaspoon salt
1 cup chopped fresh or frozen cranberries
½ cup walnuts, chopped
1½ teaspoons grated orange zest
1 partially baked tart shell (page 233)

Preheat the oven to 350 degrees.

Combine the eggs, honey, butter, orange juice, vanilla, and salt. Beat with a whisk until the mixture is smooth. Stir in the cranberries, walnuts, and orange zest.

Pour the filling into the prepared tart shell. Bake in the center of the oven for 40 to 45 minutes or until golden. Place the tart on a wire rack to cool. Let it cool completely before serving.

Cranberry, Orange, Walnut Tart

Date Walnut Tart

This tart is best made with fresh dates. There are many different varieties of dates. The medjool is large with a soft, rich flesh tasting of caramel and molasses. The barhi is smaller and very sweet, tasting of honey. There are many more varieties; these are just two that are commonly available in our markets and work well in the recipe. Serve this sweet, nutty tart with a small dollop of whipped cream and some orange slices alongside a cup of tea. // **SERVES 8 TO 10**

1 cup chopped and pitted fresh dates
3 tablespoons unbleached all-purpose flour
1 cup chopped walnuts
1 teaspoon baking powder

1 egg
½ cup honey
Pinch of salt
1 prebaked 9-inch tart shell (page 233)

Preheat the oven to 350 degrees.

Combine the chopped dates and flour in a bowl. Stir with a fork, separating the dates and coating the pieces with flour. Add the walnuts and baking powder. Stir again until well mixed.

In a separate bowl, beat the egg. Stir in the honey and salt. Add the date mixture and stir well.

Pour the filling into a prebaked tart shell. Smooth out the date mixture to fill in the tart shell.

Bake until the tart is lightly browned and the filling is set, 15 to 20 minutes.

Chocolate Pudding

This is a classic, extra-rich, chocolaty pudding—truly a comfort food dessert. Feel free to add a dash of peppermint extract or Grand Marnier. **// SERVES 6 TO 8**

6 ounces bittersweet chocolate
2 tablespoons cocoa powder
2 tablespoons cornstarch
Pinch of salt

3 cups whole milk or soy milk
½ cup honey or sugar
3 egg yolks
2 teaspoons vanilla

Melt the chocolate in the top of a double boiler or in a bowl set over a pan of boiling water. Remove from the heat to cool slightly.

Sift the cocoa, cornstarch, and salt in a heavy-bottomed saucepan. Slowly whisk in the milk, followed by the honey and then the egg yolks.

Heat the mixture over medium heat, stirring, until it is warm but not boiling. Whisk in the melted chocolate and continue whisking constantly until the mixture comes to a boil. Reduce the heat and cook, stirring, until the pudding is very thick, about 2 minutes. Remove the pan from the heat and stir in the vanilla.

Pour the pudding into a large serving bowl or individual dishes. Cover it with plastic wrap, placing the wrap directly on the pudding to prevent a skin from developing on top of the pudding. Cool for 30 minutes and then refrigerate until serving.

Garnish the pudding with fresh berries, whipped cream, or both.

Tapioca Pudding

There are three sizes of tapioca: granules, small pearl, and large pearl. Our choice for pudding is the small pearl, but the granules are quicker to cook, there is no soaking involved, and it's ready in 12 minutes. In this recipe, we use a little coconut milk diluted with water instead of all milk. When the pudding has finished cooking, pour it into small bowls. Garnish with fresh fruit if you like. Children love this. **// SERVES 8**

1 cup small pearl tapioca or tapioca granules
3 cups milk, soy milk, or almond milk
2 cups water
1 (14-ounce) can coconut milk

⅔ cup sugar
½ teaspoon ground cardamom or 1 teaspoon vanilla
Pinch of salt

Put the small pearl tapioca, milk, water, and coconut milk in a saucepan and let the tapioca soak for an hour. If you are using granules, you can skip the soaking.

Add the sugar, cardamom, and salt to the saucepan and bring the mixture to a boil, stirring, over medium-high heat. Turn the heat down to a low and simmer for approximately 13 minutes (a little less if using granules), stirring often so the tapioca does not stick.

Ladle the pudding into bowls and let it set (you don't need to cover the pudding). Serve it warm or at room temperature.

Note: You can cut this recipe in half, but it keeps for a week in the fridge.

Banana Coconut Custard

Children love this healthy custard. You can serve it with chopped-up pineapple or mango and be transported to the tropics, always a good thing in the middle of our Minnesota winters! Chop the pineapple small, though; the lovely creamy texture of the pudding doesn't want to be interrupted by chunky bites of fruit. // **SERVES 8**

1 (14-ounce) can coconut milk (low-fat is good)
1 cup soy milk, grain or nut milk, or dairy milk
2 eggs
3 ripe (not browned) bananas

⅓ cup sugar
½ teaspoon cinnamon
1 teaspoon vanilla
¼ teaspoon salt

Preheat the oven to 325 degrees. Place 8 custard cups or ramekins in a pan and pour about 1½ inches of hot water into the pan (the water should come about halfway up the sides of the ramekins).

Put all of the ingredients in a blender and puree until very smooth. Pour or ladle the mixture into the ramekins.

Bake for 30 minutes, or until the centers are cooked through.

Pumpkin Custard

You can whip this up in five minutes with the help of a blender. We love it because it's like eating pumpkin pie without the added calories of a crust. // **SERVES 6**

1 (15-ounce) can pumpkin or 2 cups pureed pumpkin
    or winter squash
2 eggs, beaten
1 cup soy milk, dairy milk, or nut or grain milk
½ cup sugar

⅓ cup raisins
¼ teaspoon ground cardamom or ginger
1 teaspoon ground cinnamon
¼ teaspoon salt
1 teaspoon vanilla

Preheat the oven to 350 degrees. Place 6 custard cups or ramekins in a pan and pour about 1½ inches of hot water into the pan (the water should come about halfway up the sides of the ramekins).

Combine all of the ingredients in a blender and puree until smooth. Pour the custard mixture into the custard cups. Bake for 30 to 35 minutes or until firm.

Apple Compote

This compote is so easy and fast. It's delicious with yogurt and granola for breakfast, as a snack, or as dessert. // **SERVES 6**

3 large apples, unpeeled and cut into thick slices
⅓ cup raisins, dried cranberries, or other dried fruit,
    chopped if large
½ cup water

1 tablespoon maple syrup, honey, or sugar
¼ teaspoon cinnamon
Pinch of salt
Chopped pecans or walnuts (optional)

Choose a large skillet so you can spread out the fruit and cook it quickly. Put all of the ingredients in the skillet and bring the mixture to a boil. Cover the pan, reduce the heat to low, and simmer for 3 to 5 minutes (some apple varieties may take a little longer to cook). Turn off the heat and let the fruit sit in the covered pan for a few more minutes. Serve warm, topped with chopped nuts, if desired.

Fruit Crisp

There are many possible fruit combinations, so feel free to experiment and use whatever is in season. Think about apple and rhubarb, pear and cranberry, and peach and cherry. In winter, when local fresh fruit is not available, try plumped dried apricots. // **SERVES 6 TO 8**

½ cup chopped nuts
¾ cup rolled oats
¾ cup unbleached all-purpose flour or a mixture of
    all-purpose flour and whole wheat pastry flour
⅓ cup packed brown sugar
¼ teaspoon salt

½ teaspoon ground cinnamon
Freshly grated nutmeg (optional)
½ cup butter or vegetable oil
6 cups fruit
Flour, cornstarch, or another thickener
⅔ cup fruit juice

Preheat the oven to 350 degrees.

Combine the nuts, oats, flour, brown sugar, salt, cinnamon, and nutmeg (if using) in a bowl. Cut the butter into small pieces, and work it in with a pastry blender or with your fingertips just until the mixture comes together and has a crumbly texture. If you are using oil instead of butter, simply stir well to combine. You can make this crisp topping in advance and store it in the refrigerator. Place it on the fruit just before putting it in the oven.

Prepare the fruit. Apples and pears can be peeled (or not), cored, and cut into slices or chunks. Stone fruits should be pitted and cut into bite-size pieces. Peaches should be peeled. Taste the fruit as you are preparing it. If the fruit is sweet, you may not need to add any sugar. If you are adding rhubarb or using tart pie cherries, you will certainly need to add some sugar; however, apples, peaches, and apricots may not need any.

If you are using juicy fruits, you will need a little flour or cornstarch to thicken the juices. Apples are generally fine without any thickener, while peaches and cherries will require 1 to 2 tablespoons of flour or cornstarch. If you need to use thickener, stir it into the juice.

Spread the prepared fruit in a 9 × 9-inch pan (or any baking dish that will hold 6 cups of fruit), pour the juice over the fruit, and place the crisp topping on top.

Bake the crisp for 45 to 50 minutes, or until the crisp topping is golden brown and the fruit is bubbling up the sides of the pan.

Variations

You can make almost any fruit into a crisp. Here are some ideas:

apple and cranberry
apple and pear
apple and rhubarb
peach
cherry, either sweet or tart
apricot and dried cherry
peaches or apricots and fresh raspberries

Fruit Crisp

Apple Sesame Kanten

Kanten is a traditional Asian fruit dessert. It is like a refreshing, creamy fruit pudding. Top it with nuts and fresh fruit. You can vary the juice used to make many different flavors. Apple juice with almond butter is a good combination, and pineapple-coconut juice with sliced oranges is very refreshing. Kanten is pretty served in goblets, and using goblets makes it easy to layer two different flavors.

// SERVES 6

4 cups apple juice
5 heaping tablespoons of agar flakes

Pour the apple juice into a saucepan. Add the agar flakes and the salt and bring the juice to a boil. Reduce the heat and simmer for 3 minutes, stirring frequently, until the agar dissolves.

Pour the mixture into a bowl and refrigerate the kanten until it sets, approximately 1½ to 2 hours.

Using a blender, blend the kanten with the tahini until it is smooth and creamy. If necessary, blend in batches. Tahini varies in thickness. If you have very thick tahini, you may need to add a little more juice to get a smooth, creamy texture. Pour the kanten into individual serving dishes.

Pinch of salt
3 tablespoons tahini

Serve the kanten cold. It's pretty served in stemmed glasses. Garnish it with fresh fruit: try berries, grapes, kiwi, or citrus.

Variations

Use apple-peach or apple-cherry juice and substitute almond butter for the tahini.

Use coconut milk in place of the tahini.

Apple Sesame Kanten

Black Cherry—Coconut Kanten

Combining black cherry juice and coconut results in a really bright and flavorful dessert. It's a fun dessert too: when we serve it to friends, guessing the flavors becomes a contest. // **SERVES 6**

6 tablespoons agar flakes
4 cups black cherry juice

Pinch of salt
1 (15-ounce) can coconut milk

Pour the cherry juice into a saucepan. Add the agar flakes and the salt and bring the juice to a boil. Reduce the heat and simmer for 3 minutes, stirring frequently, until the agar dissolves.

Pour the mixture into a bowl and refrigerate the kanten until it sets, approximately 1½ to 2 hours.

Put the kanten and the coconut milk in a blender and blend until the mixture is smooth and creamy. Pour the kanten into individual serving dishes. Serve it cold, garnished with fresh fruit.

Spoonriver still life

INDEX

INDEX

BRENDA LANGTON has been a presence in Twin Cities dining since 1972. She started her first restaurant, Cafe Kardamena, in St. Paul in 1978, and then moved it to Minneapolis and renamed it Cafe Brenda in 1986. Cafe Brenda operated until 2009. In 2006, Brenda opened Spoonriver and founded the Mill City Farmers Market. She is a senior fellow at the Center for Spirituality and Healing at the University of Minnesota and an educator and consultant on healthy eating.

MARGARET STUART is a horticulturist, landscape designer, and personal chef who has been cooking natural foods since her late teens. Langton and Stuart are coauthors of *The Cafe Brenda Cookbook*, first published in 1992 and republished by the University of Minnesota Press in 2004.

METTE NIELSEN is a Minneapolis-based food and farm photographer. She has created food images for more than twenty-five years and is an active supporter of year-round local foods in this northern climate.